Write Away

Authors
Dave Kemper, Ruth Nathan, Patrick Sebranek

Illustrator **Chris Krenzke**

WRITE SOURCE

GREAT SOURCE EDUCATION GROUP
a Houghton Mifflin Company
Wilmington, Massachusetts

2

Acknowledgements

We're grateful to many people who helped bring *Write Away* to life. First, we must thank all the students from across the country who contributed their writing models and ideas.

Also, thanks to the writers, editors, and teachers who helped make this book a reality.

Linda Bradley
Laurie Cooper
Connie Erdman
Gale Hegeman
Michelle Kerkman
Dian Lynch
Amy Nathan

Candyce Norvell
Susan Ohanian
Laura Robb
Charles Temple
Dawn Wenzel-Helnore
Sue Wind

In addition, we want to thank our Write Source team for all their help: Laura Bachman, Colleen Belmont, Carol Elsholz, Sherry Gordon, Lois Krenzke, Sue Paro, Julie Sebranek, Sandy Wagner, and Dawn Weis.

Up, Up, and Away!

The *Write Away* handbook is divided into five parts:

The Process of Writing This part helps you learn all about writing.

The Forms of Writing In here, you'll learn how to write letters, reports, stories, and more.

The Tools of Learning Reading, word study, and listening are important skills. This part covers them all.

The Proofreader's Guide When do you use periods and capital letters? You'll find out here.

The Student Almanac This part has animal facts, maps, math charts, and more!

4

Table of Contents

The PROCESS of Writing

The **FORMS** of Writing

6

The **TOOLS** of Learning

The Proofreader's GUIDE

The Student ALMANAC

BOOKS
to Grow In

There are books to grow in
and books to know in,

Books that really please you
and books that sometimes tease you,

Books you're glad you found
and books you can't put down,

Books with funny pictures
and books that make you richer,

Books with a friendly tone—
books you want, all for your own!

A Book Just for You

Write Away is a book "to grow in." It tells you all about writing and many other skills. *Write Away* will "please you" in many ways, too. It is full of fun pictures, charts, and models.

Doing Your Best Work

Think of *Write Away* as your special helper. It will help you do your best writing and learning. It is one book you will want, "all for your own!"

Write Away

The PROCESS of Writing

12

All About Writing

Starting to Write

Why are these kids smiling? They know all about writing. And guess what? They want to share some of their ideas. Let's see what they have to say.

Read, Read, Read

Lindy wrote a story about a little girl and her grandmother. She got the idea after reading Tomie dePaola's *Watch Out for the Chicken Feet in Your Soup.* Here is her advice:

Read a lot of different things. Reading gives you ideas for writing.

Pick Good Ideas

Roger just got his new cat, Henry. He wrote a letter to his aunt telling her all about Henry. Here is his writing tip:

Try Different Forms

Jenna is always writing something. She writes poems, stories, and notes. She's even writing a riddle book! Here is her advice:

Try different forms of writing. Each one teaches you something new.

Practice, Practice, Practice

Douglas likes to write. He even writes at home, when he could be watching TV! Here is the most important thing he has learned:

To become a good writer, you have to practice. Try to write every day, like me!

Share Your Writing

Ben shares his writing with friends. He likes to see how much they like his stories. He always reads their stories, too. Here is his tip:

Share your stories and poems. Sharing helps everyone write better!

Have Fun

Maybe you are just learning to write. Or maybe you already write a lot. It doesn't really matter. You only need to follow Kayla's advice:

Using the Writing Process

There are five steps in the writing process. Follow these steps when you write.

2 WRITE

Write about your subject.

Don't worry about making mistakes.

1 PLAN

Think of subjects to write about.

Choose the best one.

List ideas about your subject.

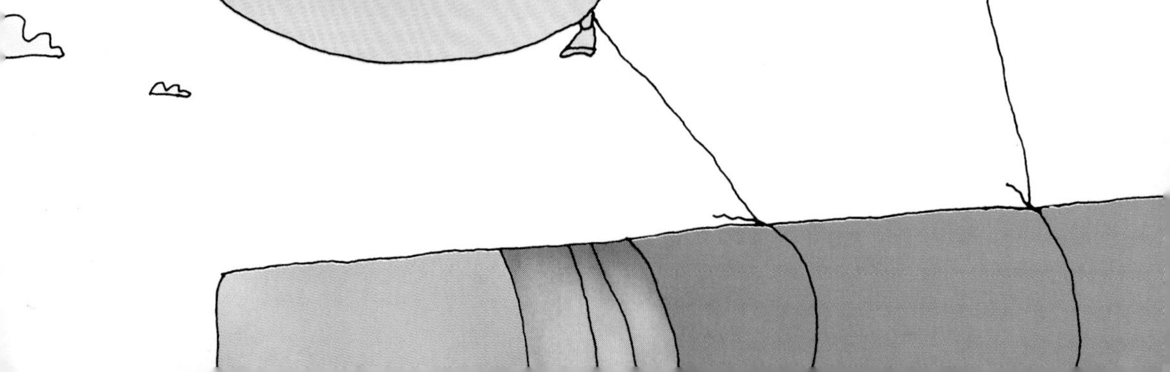

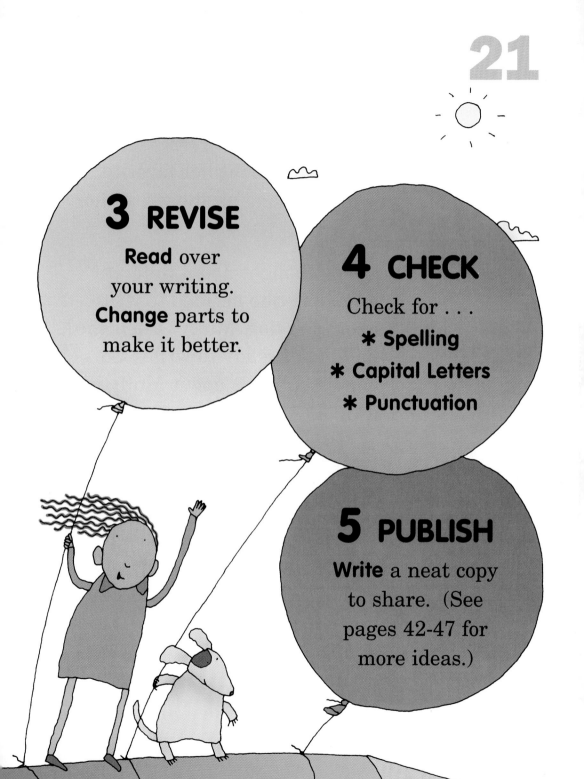

3 REVISE

Read over your writing. **Change** parts to make it better.

4 CHECK

Check for . . .
* Spelling
* Capital Letters
* Punctuation

5 PUBLISH

Write a neat copy to share. (See pages 42-47 for more ideas.)

The Writing Process in Action

Casey had to write about her favorite animal. Let's follow along as she writes her story.

PLAN

Casey thought about different animals. She decided to write about her dog, Muffy. Then she had to get ready to write. So she listed ideas about Muffy in a cluster.

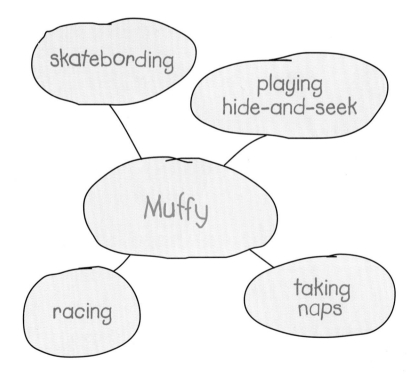

skatebording

playing hide-and-seek

Muffy

racing

taking naps

WRITE

Next, Casey wrote about her ideas. She put the sentences in the best order. This is her first draft.

My Furry Friend

I like to play with my dog muffy. I sit on the skatebord and tie it. Then Muffy pulls me. When we play hide-and-seek she always finds me. When we race, she always wins. I realy like to watch her sleep and take naps. She falls sometimes when she rolls over.

REVISE

Then Casey tried to make her writing better. Here is one idea she added:

I like to play with my dog

muffy. I sit on the skatebord
   her leash to
and tie it. Then Muffy pulls me.

4

CHECK

Casey also checked her writing for spelling, capital letters, and punctuation. Here are two things she corrected:

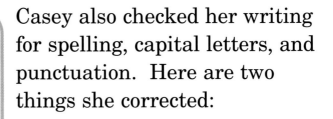

capital letter   spelling

I like to play with my dog
         skateboard
M
muffy. I sit on the ~~skatebord~~
   her leash to
and tie it. Then Muffy pulls me.

Casey wrote a neat copy of her story to share.

5

PUBLISH

My Furry Friend
I like to play with my dog Muffy. I sit on the skateboard and tie her leash to it. Then Muffy pulls me. When we play hide-and-seek, she always finds me. When we race, she always wins. I really like to watch her take naps. When she rolls over, she sometimes falls off the sofa. It is so funny!

Later on, Casey may turn her story into a picture book!

26

Prewriting and Drafting

Keeping an Idea Notebook

An **idea notebook** can be a treasure chest of writing ideas. Ideas for your notebook are all around you. You can write about recess and class trips, families and friends, special places and important happenings!

Notebook Models

Here are two example notebook pages.

Brittany's Notebook

Philip's Notebook

December 11

I learned to dive!
chin down
bend knees
arms out
fall in

shiver, shiver

December 1
   Our baby-sitter
Anne is sick. I'm
sad!

Anne

Philip used his ideas in a
letter to his grandfather.
Brittany used her ideas in
a story.

GOOD POINT

Using Your Notebook

You can use your notebook ideas when you write. Here's how:

READ over your notebook often.

PICK a good idea to write about.

TELL a partner about it.

ASK if your partner has any questions or can tell you more about the subject.

WRITE everything down.

CHOOSE a way to write about your idea. Try a letter, a poem, a story, or another form.

Read about the form in your handbook.

PLAN your first draft.

Planning Your Writing

Planning helps you write your best stories and reports. Planning has three main parts:

1. Thinking of subjects to write about

2. Choosing the best one

3. Collecting ideas for writing

Collecting Ideas

It's important to collect ideas about your subject before you write. The next page names different ways to do this.

Gather, Talk, Think

There are three main ways to collect ideas.

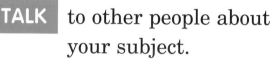

GATHER facts from books, magazines, and CD's.

TALK to other people about your subject.

THINK about your subject by trying these things:

Listing ● Just list ideas about your subject on paper.

Clustering ● Write your subject in the middle of your paper and put ideas around it. (See page 232.)

Drawing ● Plan your writing by drawing pictures about your subject.

Writing the First Draft

You pick a subject and collect ideas about it. What's next? You put those ideas into sentences. That means you write your first draft.

Putting Things in Order

Try to put all of your sentences in the best order. But don't worry about making mistakes. You can make changes later on.

Drafting TIPS

PLAN your beginning. Here are three ways to begin.

Begin with a fact:
Dogs are usually furry.

Begin with a quotation:
"My dog is the strangest beast!"

Begin with a question:
Who would want a dog like mine?

WRITE the rest of your draft. Keep going until you get all of your ideas on paper.

SKIP every other line when you write. Then you will have space to make changes and add new words.

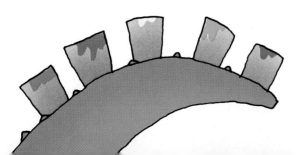

34

Revising and Checking

Revising Your Writing

Edward goes to school in Bristol, Wisconsin. He writes a lot of stories. Here is one important thing he has learned:

My writing will be good if
I make changes to parts I don't like.

Making Changes

Making changes is an important part of the writing process. When you make changes, you are **revising**. You can learn about revising on the next two pages.

Revising TIPS

Follow these tips when you revise:

READ your first draft.

LOOK for parts that could be better.

HAVE your teacher or another person read your first draft, too.

FIND OUT what your reader likes. Find out what questions he or she has.

MAKE changes in your writing.

 Cross out parts that are not needed. (Some ideas may be off the subject.)

 Change words that don't sound right.

✔ Add new words. (You may need to tell more about certain ideas in your writing.)

Checking the Three Main Parts

Make sure your writing has a good beginning, middle, and ending.

Beginning

The beginning should name your subject in an interesting way.

> I surprised my uncle and my dad when I went fishing with them.

Middle

The middle should tell about your subject.

> They always go to Eagle Lake. They think they are the best fishermen on the lake. I caught three fish. My uncle and my dad didn't catch any.

Ending

The ending should say something important about the subject.

> The next day they said I was the best fisherman!

Writing Conferences

In a **writing conference**, your teacher or a partner helps you with your writing. Here are three good reasons to have a conference:

When Planning ● To help you pick a writing subject.

When Revising ● To help you improve a first draft.

When Checking ● To help you check your writing for errors.

Working Together

Here's how revising conferences work:

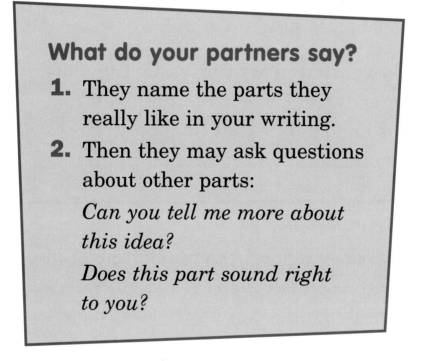

What do your partners say?

1. They name the parts they really like in your writing.
2. Then they may ask questions about other parts:

   Can you tell me more about this idea?

   Does this part sound right to you?

What should you do?

1. Listen to what your partners say.
2. Answer any questions.
3. Try to make your first draft better.

Checking for Errors

When is your writing ready to publish? It is ready after you have checked it for errors and made a neat final copy. Checking for errors is called **proofreading**.

Work Carefully!

It's easy to miss errors. So you have to check your writing very carefully. Use the checklist and tips on the next page to help you proofread.

Proofreading TIPS

READ your writing aloud. Then you can listen for errors.

TOUCH each word with your pencil. This will help you check for spelling.

FIND a helper. Have your teacher or someone else check your writing, too.

Proofreading Checklist

✔ Did you capitalize the first word in each sentence?

✔ Did you capitalize names?

✔ Did you put a period, a question mark, or an exclamation point after each sentence?

✔ Did you spell your words correctly?

Publishing Your Writing

Publishing is sharing the final copy of your writing. To publish, you can read your stories to your classmates. You can also post your writing on a bulletin board.

Sharing Your Work

This chapter lists many other ways to publish. You will also learn about adding pictures and making books.

Publishing Ideas

MAKE a picture book for one of
your stories.

PUT TOGETHER a class book of stories
or poems.

ACT OUT your story or play.

PUT ON a puppet show.

DESIGN a birthday or holiday card
using your own poem.

PRINT a class newspaper.

READ your report to the
parent/teacher group.

SEND one of your best stories or
poems to a magazine. (Ask
your teacher for help.)

Adding Pictures

It can be fun to draw pictures to go with your writing. You can draw them before, while, or after you write.

Drawing One Picture

Sometimes one picture is all you need. Auburn wrote a poem about a bird called a quetzal (*say* ket-`säl).

Quetzal

I am quetzal
living in the canopy.
My tail feathers
are three feet long.
In one day
I can eat
43 kinds of fruit.
My body hovers
like a hummingbird.
I'm an endangered animal.

Drawings in a Picture Book

Sometimes you can make a whole picture book. Jamie made a picture book for his all-about-me story. Each page had one or two sentences and a picture. Here is one of his pages:

I surprised my uncle and my dad when I went fishing with them.

Binding a Book

Book Design

Books can be different shapes and sizes.

Steps to Follow

- Make a front and back cover.
- Design a title page.
- Stack all the pages between the covers.
- Put your book together with yarn, rings, staples, or string.

Book Cover and Title Page

Example Cover

Example Title Page

48

Sentences and Paragraphs

Writing Sentences

A **sentence** is a group of words that tells a complete idea. Every sentence has a naming part and a telling part.

The Naming Part	The Telling Part
Aunt Jill	sleeps.
The boys	play in the yard.

Sentence Parts

Subject

The naming part is also called the **subject**. The subject names who or what the sentence is about.

Grandpa sings.

Verb

The telling part is also called the **verb**. The verb usually tells what the subject is doing.

Grandpa sings.

Other Parts

We usually add words to the subject or verb to make the idea clearer.

Grandpa sings in the shower.

Subject/Verb Agreement

The <u>subject</u> and <u>verb</u> must go together in a sentence.

Singular subjects go with singular verbs. (Singular means "one.")

<u>Jenny</u> <u>loves</u> milk.

Plural subjects go with plural verbs. (Plural means "more than one.")

My <u>cousins</u> <u>love</u> juice.

Sentence Problem

Try not to run too many sentences together using the words "and then."

Too many "and then's":

> **Jose ate his lunch really fast and then he jumped up and then he ran outside.**

Better:

> **Jose ate his lunch really fast. Then he jumped up and ran outside.**

52

Writing Longer Sentences

Do you know how to write longer sentences? You can combine two or three shorter ones.

Two sentences:

Polar bears swim fast.
Polar bears catch fish.

One longer sentence:

**Polar bears swim fast
and catch fish.**

The next page shows you how to combine sentences.

Combine Subjects

Two sentences:

Foxes live near the North Pole.
Wolves live near the North Pole.

Longer sentence with two subjects:

**Foxes and wolves live
near the North Pole.**

Combine Verbs

Three sentences:

Penguins dive in water.
They leap in water.
They paddle in water.

Longer sentence with three verbs:

**Penguins dive, leap, and
paddle in water.**

You can combine other
words, too.

**Walruses look big,
fat, and sleepy.**

Writing Paragraphs

Writing is many things. It is describing a subject or giving information. It is sharing a story or giving reasons.

Sharing and Telling

You can do all of these things in a paragraph. This chapter shows you how to write a describing paragraph, plus much more.

What Is a Paragraph?

A **paragraph** is three or more sentences about the same subject. All paragraphs have a beginning, a middle, and an ending.

Beginning

The first sentence is called the **topic sentence**. It names the subject. (The first sentence in a paragraph is indented.)

Middle

The middle sentences are called the **body**. They tell about the subject.

Ending

The last sentence is called the **closing sentence**. It gives an interesting idea about the subject.

Reading model paragraphs helps you write them. You can get started by reading the model on the next page.

Student MODEL

In this model, Michael decribes his favorite sandwich.

My Best Sandwich

Topic Sentence

Toasted cheese sandwiches are great.

Body

They smell buttery and look golden brown. When you bite into one, you can see the melted yellow cheese. Toasted cheese sandwiches taste crunchy on the outside and creamy in the middle.

Closing Sentence

I could eat one every day!

Writing a Describing Paragraph

1 PLAN

Pick a Subject

Pick a person, place, or thing to describe.

Collect Ideas

List ideas about your subject. How does it look, sound, or smell?

2 WRITE

Write the Three Parts

Name your subject in the topic sentence. Tell about it in the middle sentences. End with a closing idea that's interesting.

3 REVISE

Check Your First Draft

* Do all of your sentences describe the subject?
* Are your sentences in the best order?

4 CHECK

Check for Errors

Check your sentences for capital letters, punctuation, and spelling. Then write a neat final copy.

Remember to indent the first line in your paragraph.

More Models

Giving Information

In this paragraph, Kumal gives important information about plants and their roots.

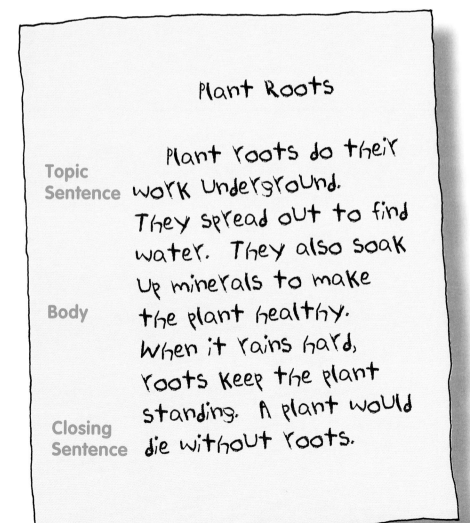

Plant Roots

Topic Sentence Plant roots do their work underground. They spread out to find water. They also soak up minerals to make **Body** the plant healthy. When it rains hard, roots keep the plant standing. A plant would **Closing Sentence** die without roots.

Sharing a Story

In this paragraph, Juana shares a story about visiting a park.

Park Adventure

Topic Sentence
My dad and I went to Blue Hills Park. We hiked to the top of a big hill above the clouds! Then we explored Treasure Cave.

Body
It was scary and dark inside. Later, we saw three fat raccoons.

Closing Sentence
We had a lot of fun and will visit the park again!

Giving Reasons

In this paragraph, Dee Dee gives reasons why her aunt is so special.

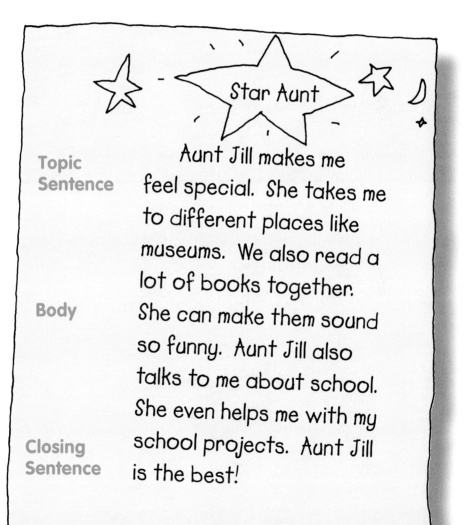

Topic Sentence

Body

Closing Sentence

Star Aunt

Aunt Jill makes me feel special. She takes me to different places like museums. We also read a lot of books together. She can make them sound so funny. Aunt Jill also talks to me about school. She even helps me with my school projects. Aunt Jill is the best!

The FORMS of Writing

Personal Writing

Writing in Journals

In a **journal**, you can write about how you feel and what you think. It is your very own writing place!

A Present a Day

Josh says, "Writing in a journal is like giving yourself a present every day!" Josh is ready to help you start your own journal. Just follow along.

Journal-Writing TIPS

WRITE in your journal every day.

KEEP your eyes and ears open for ideas.

DON'T WORRY about your spelling, but try to write neatly.

DRAW pictures whenever you want to because drawing helps you think.

REREAD your journal a lot. You will get good ideas for other writing you do.

Ideas for Journal Writing

Josh writes about events.

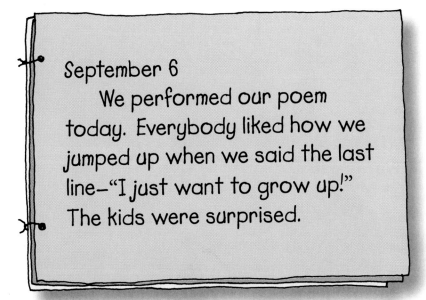

September 6
    We performed our poem today. Everybody liked how we jumped up when we said the last line—"I just want to grow up!" The kids were surprised.

Josh writes about learning.

January 30
   Here are some good habits
we're learning about in school.
   – eat healthful foods
   – play a lot
   – relax
   Another idea is
to be nice to other kids!

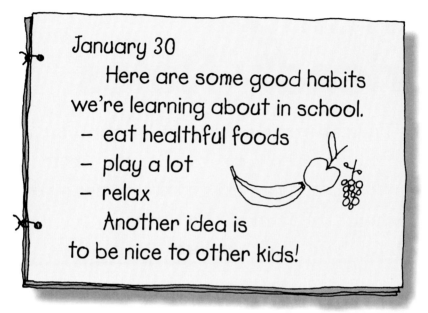

He also writes about his reading.

March 8
   I want to write a book
just like Horrible Harry in 2B.
I'm going to read it again. The
characters sound just like real
kids. I want my characters to
sound real, too!

Writing Friendly Notes

You can write notes to a lot of people. You can write to your friends, your mom, or your dad. You can even write notes to your teacher. People like to get friendly notes. It tells them that you care.

Notes Are Easy

To get started, write a note to a friend. Put it in a special place where he or she will find it. You may soon get a note back!

Cool Ideas for Notes

Tell Something You Know

Dear Josie,

An anteater eats 30,000 ants a day. We need one at our house.

Ha ha,
Tanya

Send Good Wishes

Dear Joe,

I'm sorry you broke your leg. We miss you. I hope you'll be back soon.

Your friend,
Eric

Say Thank You

Dear Uncle Mike,

Thank you for the calculator. You always know what I need! Now I can check my math homework.

Love,
Sarah

Share a Message

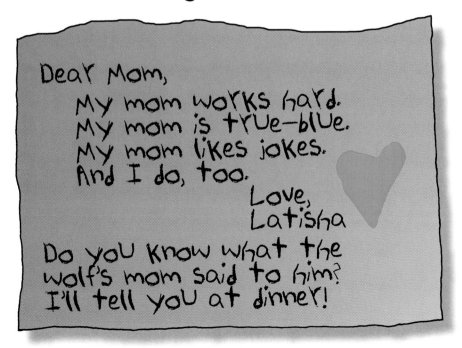

Dear Mom,
My mom works hard.
My mom is true-blue.
My mom likes jokes.
And I do, too.
Love,
Latisha
Do you know what the wolf's mom said to him? I'll tell you at dinner!

Fun Note Ideas

Here are two ways to have fun with notes.

Cut out a shape for your note.

Lee,
Meet me at the park after school.
Saul

Add a picture to your note.

Linda,
My mom says you can stay over on Friday. We can have pizza. Ask your mom.

Beth

Writing Friendly Letters

Friendly letters are a lot like friendly notes. But friendly letters travel! They can reach friends and relatives faraway.

Reaching Out

Write a letter and put a smile on someone's face. John did! Read his letter on the next page. Then we will help you write your own letter.

Student MODEL

Friendly letters have five parts. The parts are marked in this letter.

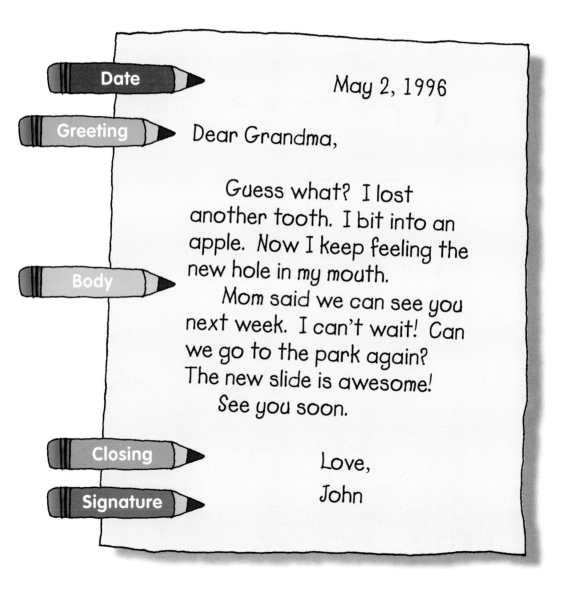

Date May 2, 1996

Greeting Dear Grandma,

Body

Guess what? I lost another tooth. I bit into an apple. Now I keep feeling the new hole in my mouth.

Mom said we can see you next week. I can't wait! Can we go to the park again? The new slide is awesome!

See you soon.

Closing Love,

Signature John

Steps in Writing a Friendly Letter

1

PLAN

Pick Someone to Write To

* a relative
* a close friend

List Ideas

List two or three things you want to say.

I lost my tooth.
We are coming
to visit.
Can we go
to the park?

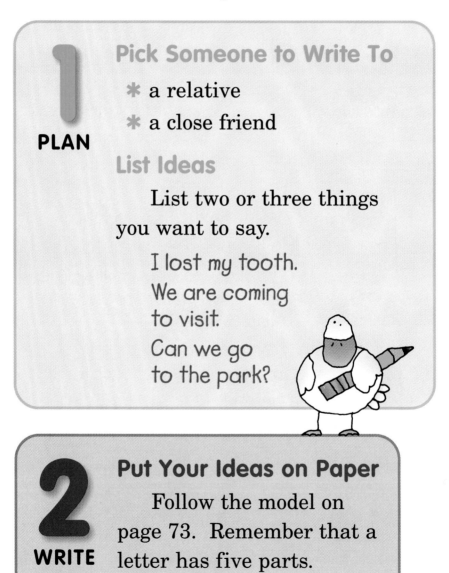

2

WRITE

Put Your Ideas on Paper

Follow the model on page 73. Remember that a letter has five parts.

3 REVISE

Check Your First Draft

* Did you say all of the important things?
* Did you remember the five parts of a letter?

4 CHECK

Check for Errors

✔ Check your sentences for capital letters.
✔ Check for punctuation and spelling.
✔ Make sure your letter looks nice.

To send your letter, see pages 100-101 for help.

Writing All-About-Me Stories

All-about-me stories tell about things that happen to you. They can be funny or surprising. They can be long or short. They can be old or new.

Getting Started

You can read an all-about-me story on the next page. Then we'll show you how to write your own story to share.

Dad

Student MODEL

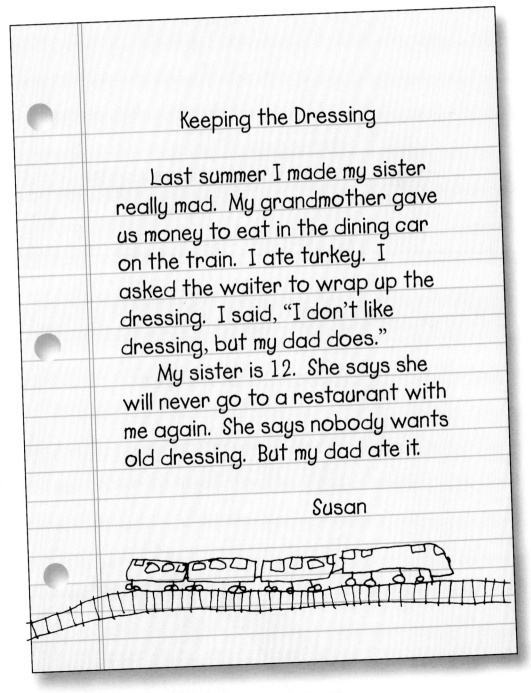

Keeping the Dressing

Last summer I made my sister really mad. My grandmother gave us money to eat in the dining car on the train. I ate turkey. I asked the waiter to wrap up the dressing. I said, "I don't like dressing, but my dad does."

My sister is 12. She says she will never go to a restaurant with me again. She says nobody wants old dressing. But my dad ate it.

Susan

Steps in Writing an All-About-Me Story

1 PLAN

List Ideas

List two or three things that happened to you.

I broke *my arm* on vacation.

I ate dinner on a train.

I lost *my cat.*

Choose a Story Idea

Pick one idea from your list to write about.

Talk About Your Idea

Tell your story out loud to a friend.

2 WRITE

Start with a Bang

Here is Susan's first sentence:

"Last summer I made my sister really mad."

Write the Rest of the Story

Tell all of the parts.

3 REVISE

Read Your First Draft

Did you forget anything?

Make Changes

Add any missing parts.

4 CHECK

Check for Errors

Check your sentences for end punctuation, capital letters, and spelling. Write a neat final copy.

Subject
Writing

Writing About Books

Reading a good book is fun. Sharing your ideas about the book can be fun, too. You can share your ideas in a book review.

Getting Started

This chapter will help you write a book review. It includes two models for you to read and writing guidelines for you to follow.

MODEL **Book Review**

Here is Jackie's review of a book with a make-believe story. Each paragraph answers a main question.

1. What is the book about?

2. Why do I like this book?

Julius the Baby of the World

Julius the Baby of the World is a book by Kevin Henkes. This book tells the story of Lily. She is mad at her baby brother Julius because everybody thinks he is so great. In the end, Lily changes her feelings about him.

I think this book is very funny. I laughed at Lily a lot. And I know how she feels. Sometimes I get mad at my baby brother.

MODEL **Book Review**

Here is Joshua's review of a true book. Each paragraph answers a main question.

1. What is the book about?

2. Why do I like this book?

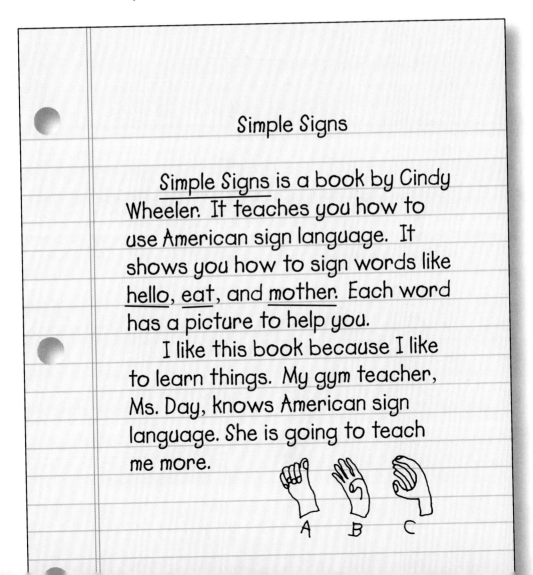

Simple Signs

Simple Signs is a book by Cindy Wheeler. It teaches you how to use American sign language. It shows you how to sign words like hello, eat, and mother. Each word has a picture to help you.

I like this book because I like to learn things. My gym teacher, Ms. Day, knows American sign language. She is going to teach me more.

A   B   C

Writing a Book Review

1 PLAN

Pick a Book

Choose a book that you like a lot.

Think About the Book

What happens in this book? What is the best part? (You could draw a picture.)

2 WRITE

Answer Two Main Questions

* What is the book about?
* Why do I like it?

3

REVISE

Check Your First Draft

* Did you answer the two questions?
* Did you include all of the important ideas in your answers?

4

CHECK

Check for Errors
Check your sentences for capital letters, punctuation, and spelling. Then write a neat final copy.

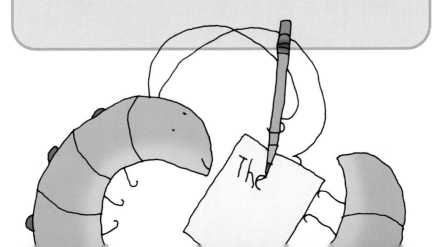

Making Counting Books

Counting jingles are fun to say:

One, **two**, **buckle my shoe.**
Three, **four**, **shut the door.**
Five, **six**, **pick up sticks. . . .**

And counting books are fun to make!

Numbers Plus!

Counting books use numbers . . . of course. There are special words and pictures to go with the numbers, too.

Student MODEL

Here is the first page in Shari's counting book called *Circus Fun.* (She counts by 2's.)

2 Amazing Acrobats

Here is the second page in Shari's counting book.

4 Crazy Clowns

Shari has chosen words that begin with the same sound (<u>C</u>razy <u>C</u>lowns). This makes her book fun to read.

Making a Counting Book

1 PLAN

Pick a Number Pattern

* 1, 2, 3, 4, . . .
* 2, 4, 6, 8, . . .
* 5, 10, 15, 20, . . .

Pick a Subject

What will you write and draw about?

Shari picked the circus.

Plan Your Book

What types of ideas will you put on each page?

Shari named different circus performers.

2 WRITE

State Your Ideas

* Use special words:

  2 Amazing Acrobats

* Or use sentences:

  Two acrobats did flips.

Draw Your Pictures

3 REVISE

Check Your Work

* Do all of the numbers fit the pattern?

* Did you use the best words and pictures?

4 CHECK

Check for Errors

Look carefully for spelling errors. Then make a neat final copy of your book.

Writing with Numbers and Rhyme

Here's how Stephen used numbers and rhyme in a fun way.

His First Step ● He made two lists.

Numbers	Rhyming Words
one	bun, fun, run, sun
two	boo, new, zoo
three	bee, knee, see, tree

His Second Step ● Then he wrote two sentences for each number.

Numbers and Rhyme

First there's one.
Get ready for fun.

Next comes two.
Let's go to the zoo.

Writing News Stories

Students in Room 20 wanted to share their writing with other classes. So they made a newspaper called the *Record*. It is filled with stories about school life.

Read All About It!

You can read one of the stories on the next page. Then you can learn how to write your own news story.

MODEL News Story

THE RECORD

New Food Plan ❶

by Beth Cramer ❷

❸ We now have two choices for hot lunch.

❹ The cooks keep a record of the most popular choices. So far, pizza is the first choice. Hot dogs are second.

Ms. Hunt is our food director. She said, "We want students to eat all of their food and enjoy it." ❺

Parts of a News Story

❶ The **headline** names the story.

❷ The **byline** shows the author.

❸ The **beginning** gives the most important idea.

❹ The **middle** tells more about the story.

❺ The **ending** gives the reader an idea to remember.

Writing a News Story

1 PLAN

List Ideas

List two or three important events:
- *your class play*
- *the new lunch plan*

Pick One Idea

Choose the best idea for your news story.

Collect Facts

Here are ways to collect facts about your idea:

* Talk to people about it.
* Read about it.
* Watch it in action.

2 WRITE — Write the Story

* Give the most important idea in the first sentence.
* Give other facts in the middle.
* End with an interesting idea.

3 REVISE — Check the First Draft

Did you include all the facts?

4 CHECK — Check for Errors

Check your story for spelling, capital letters, and periods. Write a neat final copy.

Writing Business Letters

Grown-ups write business letters all the time. They send for information. They order things. They try to solve problems.

Sending Out

You can learn to write business letters, too. Then you can send for information for school and do other neat things. We will show you how in this chapter.

Zoo Director
Box 1012
Simso IA
53042

US MAIL

Letter-Writing TIPS

KNOW why you are writing your letter.

- Do you need information for school?
- Do you want to join a club?
- Do you want to order something?

FIND out who to write to.

STATE your ideas clearly and neatly.

SOUND polite and thankful. In most cases, you will be writing to a grown-up.

FOLLOW the form for a business letter and for the address on an envelope. (See pages 98-100.)

USE your best handwriting. (If you can, type your letter on a computer.)

CHECK the letter for errors before sending it.

Six Parts of a Business Letter

1 **Heading:** Give your address and the date.

2 **Inside Address:** Write the name and address of the person or company you are writing to.

3 **Salutation:** Use a title, or **Ms.** for women and **Mr.** for men.

Dear Officer Friendly:

Dear Ms. Cheng:

4 **Body:** Explain what you need.

5 **Closing:** Use **Sincerely** followed by a comma (,).

6 **Signature:** Write your name under the closing.

MODEL Business Letter

1 609 Chicago Street
Baytown, NY 10303
March 30, 1996

2 Officer Friendly
Baytown Police Department
100 Main Street
Baytown, NY 10303

3 Dear Officer Friendly:

My name is Michael Sanders, and I am in second grade. We are going to study bike safety. It will be next week.

4 I think you know a lot about bike safety. Please send me your information. It is my job for the class.

Thank you.

5 Sincerely,

6 Michael Sanders

Sending Your Letter

Addressing the Envelope

- Use all capital letters and no punctuation marks.
- Use the post office abbreviations for states and streets. (See pages 258-259.)
- Put your address in the top left-hand corner.
- Put the stamp in the top right-hand corner.

MICHAEL SANDERS
609 CHICAGO ST
BAYTOWN NY 10303

U.S.

OFFICER FRIENDLY
BAYTOWN POLICE DEPARTMENT
100 MAIN ST
BAYTOWN NY 10303

Folding Your Letter

- Fold your letter into three equal parts.
- Put your letter into the envelope. Then seal the envelope.
- Check the address and stamp.
- Mail your letter!

...nd I
...e going to
...l be next
week.

I think you know a lot about bike safety. Please send me your information. It is my job for the class.

Thank you.

Sincerely,
Michael Sanders

Writing Directions

Everyone is good at something. You may be good at hitting a softball. Or you may make the best peanut butter and jelly sandwich. Yum!

Step-by-Step

In this chapter, we will show you how to write **directions**. Then you can explain how your skill is done. Or you can explain how to get to a special place.

Two Kinds of Directions

Making a PB & J Sandwich

It's easy to make a peanut butter and jelly sandwich. First, spread peanut butter on one piece of bread. Then, spread jelly on the other piece. Next, put the two pieces of bread together. Keep the peanut butter and jelly on the inside. Last, cut the sandwich in half and start eating!

How to Get to the Nurse's Office

1. Go out of our classroom and turn left.
2. Walk to the stairs and go down.
3. Turn right at the bottom of the stairs.
4. Walk a long way down the hall.
5. Stop at Room 104, the nurse's office.

Writing a Set of Directions

1 PLAN

Pick a Subject

Choose something you like to do or make. (Or choose a special place to go.)

Think About It

* What will you say in your directions?
* What steps will you give?

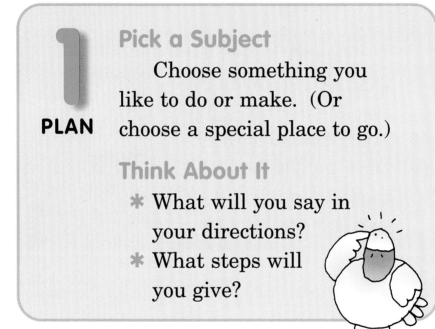

2 WRITE

Write the Directions

* Use time words like *first* and *then* to make your directions clear.
* Or use numbers before each step.

3

REVISE

Check the Directions

* Did you include all the steps?
* Are the steps in the right order?

4

CHECK

Check for Errors

Check your sentences for spelling, capital letters, and periods. Then write a neat copy of your directions to share.

You can add pictures to your directions, too.

Making Posters

Posters are like BIG notes. Some posters tell about special events. They tell where and when an event is going to happen. Posters may also say something important about a subject.

Post a Big Note!

Study the posters on the next two pages. Then learn how to make your own.

MODEL Telling About an Event

MODEL Sharing an Idea

Poster-Making TIPS

A good poster needs a strong picture and just a few words. Here are some tips to follow:

GATHER all your facts.

THINK of a main idea to put in your picture.

PLAN your poster on a small piece of paper.

- Use all the space.
- Put your title in big letters.

DRAW a copy of your plan onto a large piece of paper.

SHOW your work to a classmate. Maybe your friend will give you an idea.

CHECK your spelling and facts.

COLOR your poster.

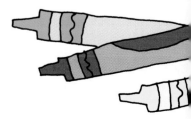

Research Writing

Using the Library

A library is packed with books. There are books about neat places and wild animals. There are books full of great stories and much more!

Looking and Learning

This chapter talks about the different kinds of books. It also shows you how to find books and how to use them. All of these ideas will help you use the library.

Learning About Library Books

Fiction Books

A **fiction book** is make-believe. The story did not really happen. The author made it up.

Look for It Fiction books have their own place in the library. They are usually found in ABC order by the author's last name.

Nonfiction Books

A **nonfiction book** is true. Nonfiction books give facts about subjects like the rain forest and airplanes.

Look for It Nonfiction books are put on the shelves in number order. They have "call numbers" printed on them. (See page 116 to learn more about this.)

Biographies

A **biography** is a true book about the life of an important person like a president or an inventor.

Look for It Biographies have their own place in the library, too. They are in ABC order by the last name of the person the book is about.

Reference Books

A **reference book** has lots of facts and information. Encyclopedias and dictionaries are reference books.

Look for It Reference books have a special place in the library. Your teacher or librarian will show you where they are.

DICTIONARY

Finding Library Books

Card Catalog

The **card catalog** names the books in your library. A book usually has a title card, a subject card, and an author card in this catalog. All of the cards in the catalog are in ABC order.

Example Title Card

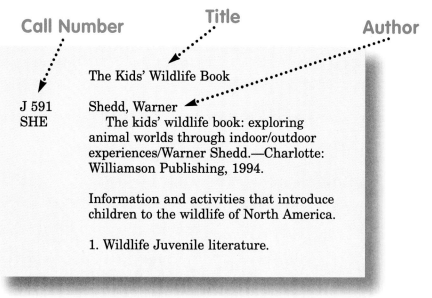

Call Number   Title   Author

The Kids' Wildlife Book

J 591   Shedd, Warner
SHE   The kids' wildlife book: exploring
             animal worlds through indoor/outdoor
             experiences/Warner Shedd.—Charlotte:
             Williamson Publishing, 1994.

             Information and activities that introduce
             children to the wildlife of North America.

             1. Wildlife Juvenile literature.

You can look in the card catalog for a title, a subject, or an author. If a title begins with *A, An,* or *The,* look up the next word.

Computer Catalog

Many libraries have their card catalogs on a computer. The computer shows you the same information you would find in a card catalog. You just type in a title, an author, or a keyword. A **keyword** works like a subject card.

```
Author:     Shedd, Warner
Title:      The Kids' Wildlife Book
Published:  Carlotte: Williamson
            Publishing, 1994.
Subject:    Wildlife Juvenile literature
Call number:            Status:
J 591 SHE               Not checked out
Location:
Children's
```

Using Call Numbers

To find nonfiction books, you need to know the **call number**. *The Kids' Wildlife Book* by Warner Shedd has this call number: J591
                                                          SHE

Below, you can see where this book fits on the shelf.

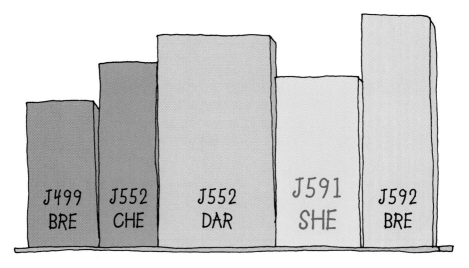

J499 BRE | J552 CHE | J552 DAR | J591 SHE | J592 BRE

GOOD POINT Always ask your librarian or teacher for help if you cannot find a book. Either one can help you become "library smart"!

Using Nonfiction Books

Nonfiction books are easier to use when you understand their parts. Here are the main parts in nonfiction books.

At the Beginning

- The **title page** is the first page. It gives the book title and the author's name.
- The **table of contents** names each chapter and tells what page it starts on.

In the Middle

- The **body** is the main part of the book. It includes all of the chapters.

At the End

- The **glossary** explains special words used in the book.
- The **index** is an ABC list of all the topics in the book. It gives the page number where each topic is found.

Writing Reports

John Walker learned three things about his favorite dinosaur: *how big it was, what it ate,* and *where it lived.* Then he wrote a report about this information. You can read his report on page 123.

Finding and Sharing

Do you know how to find information about a subject? We will show you how in this chapter. We will also show you ways to report on what you find out.

Finding Information for Reports

Select a Good Subject

- Start with a large topic you are studying. It could be dinosaurs.
- List ideas about the topic that interest you. You can look in books or ask friends for ideas.
- Choose the most interesting idea to be your subject.

Think About Your Subject

- Write two or three questions you have about your subject.
- Put your questions on note cards or on a gathering grid. (See page 121 for a model grid.)

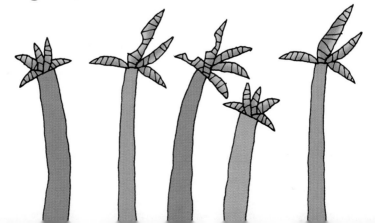

Learn About Your Subject

- You can look in many places to learn about your subject:

    books, tapes, magazines, interviews, CD's, the Internet

- Try to use more than one source of information.

- Write answers to your questions as you read and learn. Do this on note cards or on a gathering grid.

Example Note Card

What did Brachiosaurus eat?

- leaves from trees

- water plants

Using a Gathering Grid

A **gathering grid** helps you organize the information you collect about your subject.

Getting Started

USE a big piece of paper.

DRAW lines to make a grid.

WRITE your questions and answer them.

Brachiosaurus	Book	Tape and Picture Set
How big was it?	75-80 ft. long and 40 ft. high	taller than a four-story building
What did it eat?	tree leaves	water plants

 If you think of new questions or find other facts, write them on your grid.

Writing a Classroom Report

You can write about your information in a classroom report. This page will help you. Also see John's report on the next page.

Beginning   Your first paragraph should name your subject in an interesting way. John starts by asking a question. You could also give an important fact.

Middle   Use the information from your notes to write the main part. Each paragraph should answer one question.

Ending   Tell what you have learned or how you feel about the subject.

Remember to check your report for errors before you write a final copy.

MODEL Classroom Report

Brachiosaurus
by John Walker

What's the longest, tallest, and heaviest dinosaur that ever lived? It was the Brachiosaurus.

Beginning

Brachiosaurus was 75-80 feet long and 40 feet high. That was taller than a four-story building! It had a long neck. It could reach the top of 40-foot trees.

Middle

Brachiosaurus ate water plants and leaves from trees. It must have eaten a lot. One Brachiosaurus was as heavy as 10 elephants.

Brachiosaurus lived in the western part of North America. Maybe I'll find a fossil someday since I live in California.

Ending

Example Picture

More Reporting Ideas

This list shows other ways to report on information. You can probably think of many more!

LIST POEM Write a poem that gives facts about your subject. (See the next page.)

STORY Write a story about your subject. (See the next page.)

POSTER Make a poster about your subject. (See pages 106-109.)

PICTURE DICTIONARY Report on your subject in a picture dictionary. (See pages 126-129.)

ORAL REPORT Tell important facts about your subject. Have pictures or examples that show your facts, too.

MODEL
List Poem

Garrett lists many facts about an ocelot in his poem.

Ocelot

I am an ocelot.
You can find me climbing
Up the trees
Trying to find my prey.
Some things I eat
Are snakes and lizards.
You can only find me
Doing this at night.
I am four feet long.
My big eyes help me see.

MODEL
Story

Here is the start of Lauren's story about an otter.

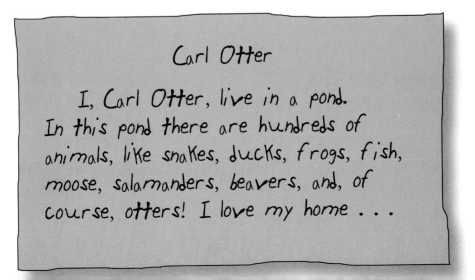

Carl Otter

I, Carl Otter, live in a pond.
In this pond there are hundreds of
animals, like snakes, ducks, frogs, fish,
moose, salamanders, beavers, and, of
course, otters! I love my home . . .

Making Picture Dictionaries

To make a **picture dictionary**, you need to do three things:

1. Put a set of words in ABC order.

2. Write something about each word.

3. Draw a picture for each word.

Picking a Subject

A picture dictionary can be about anything from dogs to dinosaurs to kites. This chapter will help you make your own picture dictionary.

kite

Student MODEL

Tony did a picture dictionary about motor vehicles. You can see some of his work on the next two pages.

BUS

A bus has many wheels. People ride buses to get around in a city. Some buses can hold 70 people.

MOTORCYCLE

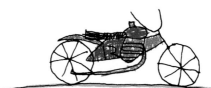

A motorcycle has two wheels. People ride motorcycles for fun. One or two people can ride on a motorcycle.

PICKUP

A pickup has four wheels. People haul things in pickups. A pickup usually has room for two people.

Dictionary-Making TIPS

PICK a subject you really like. Here are some ideas:

> wild animals
> motor vehicles
> dinosaurs
> musical instruments

LIST words for your dictionary. Each word should be about the subject.

SELECT the best words. (You don't have to use all of them.)

PUT the words in ABC order.

FIND facts for each word.

SET UP your dictionary. Each page should have a word, sentences, and a picture.

CHECK your pages for spelling errors.

MAKE a final copy with a cover. (See pages 46-47 for help.)

Story Writing

Writing Circle Stories

Jane loves circle stories. A **circle story** begins and ends in the same place. Jane thinks it's fun to figure out how the author will get back to the beginning.

Reading and Writing

One day, Jane's teacher read *If You Give a Mouse a Cookie* by Laura Numeroff. After hearing it, Jane had a great idea for a circle story. You can read it on the next page.

Student MODEL

Here is Jane's circle story:

If You Give a Kitten Some String!

If you give a kitten some string . . .
She'll play with it.
Then she'll get all tangled up!
Then she'll go in the kitchen so you can
    get her untangled!
Then she'll leave the string there
    because she's tired, and she'll lie on
    your bed!
Then she'll want you to read her a story.
Then the story will get boring, so she'll
    look for some string to play with.
And, chances are, she'll get all tangled
    up again!

Jane drew a picture for each main idea in her story.

Story-Writing TIPS

READ more circle stories. That will help you write your own. Here are two books to read:

Millions of Cats by Wanda Ga'g
Rosie's Walk by Pat Hutchins

MAKE a map of ideas for your story. Here is the start of Jane's story map:

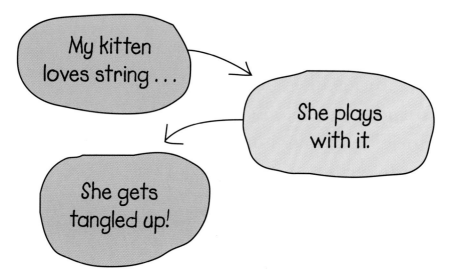

My kitten loves string . . .

She plays with it.

She gets tangled up!

WRITE your story and draw your pictures.

CHECK your story for errors before you share it.

Writing Add-On Stories

Stories like "The Very Enormous Turnip" and "Stone Soup" are called add-on stories. Add-on stories are fun to read and fun to write.

The Working Parts

In an **add-on story**, the main character has a problem. One by one, different characters are added to the story. A surprise happens in the end, and the problem is solved.

Student MODEL

Here is Connie's add-on story:

Dance Steps

Connie really wanted to tap-dance. She tried, but she couldn't do it.

So she asked Karen, her baby-sitter, to teach her. Karen said, "Sorry, I only know how to line-dance."

Then Connie asked her friend Lizzy. But Lizzy said, "Sorry, I only know how to square-dance."

Next, Connie asked her neighbor Mr. Cosford. But he said, "Sorry, I only know how to polka."

Connie thought she would never learn. She asked one last person, her dad. He said, "Sure, I'll teach you how to tap-dance."

So Connie and her dad danced and danced. Everyone was so surprised. No one knew her dad could tap-dance!

Writing an Add-On Story

1 PLAN

Pick a Main Character

List Story Ideas or Problems

Here is Connie's list:

choosing a pet

✔ learning to tap-dance

fixing a bike

Choose One Problem for Your Story

List Add-On Characters

Connie listed people she knew:

baby-sitter   dad

Mr. Cosford   Lizzy

2 WRITE

Begin Your Story
Name the main character and tell about his or her problem.

Keep It Going
Add one character at a time to try to help.

3 REVISE

Check Your First Draft
* Did your characters say fun or interesting things?
* Did you save a surprise for the end?

4 CHECK

Check for Errors
Check your sentences for errors before you write a final copy.

Writing Fables

A **fable** is a story that teaches a lesson. You may know the fable about the tortoise and the hare. The slow tortoise wins a race because the hare rests. In the end, we learn this lesson: *slow but steady wins the race.*

Your Turn

You can write a fable, too. First read the model on the next page. Then we'll show you the steps.

MODEL Fable

The Wolf and the Kid

A mother goat and her kid lived in the woods. She had to go out to get some food, so she told her little kid to lock the door and not let anyone in. The wolf was hiding nearby and heard her. After she had gone, he went to the door and tapped lightly. The kid bleated, "Who's there?"

"It's your mother, sonny. Open the door," said the wolf in a high, squeaky voice.

The kid went around and peeked through the window. "You say you are my mother," said the kid, as he giggled. "You almost sound like her, too. But you look like a wolf to me!" And he left the door bolted.

Lesson: Mother knows best.

Writing a Fable

1 PLAN

List Characters

Pick one or two main characters for your fable. (See the list on the next page.)

Think About the Lesson

Which character will learn a lesson? What will the lesson be? (See the list on the next page for ideas.)

Think About the Setting

Where will your story take place? In a woods? At the beach? In a farmer's field?

Fable Characters

Fable characters are almost always animals. Here are some of the animals found in fables:

donkey	lion	rooster
fox	mouse	sheep
frog	owl	snake
goat	peacock	turtle
horse	rabbit	wolf

Fable Lessons

Here are some lessons to think about:

- Do not trust someone who only praises you.
- Little friends can be great friends.
- Be prepared.
- Don't count on something until it happens.

WRITE

Start Your Fable

Tell where the story takes place. Have your characters meet and talk.

Keep the Fable Going

* Show that one character has a problem or may need to learn a lesson.

* Make something happen. The characters may try to outsmart each other.

End Your Fable

Help the readers learn the lesson.

Use the model as a guide when you write.

3 REVISE

Share Your Fable

Ask your partner to listen for two things:

- a favorite part
- the lesson in the fable

Make Changes

Did you miss any parts? Did your partner have any questions?

4 CHECK

Check for Errors

✔ Check your fable for spelling, capital letters, and end punctuation.

✔ Then write a neat final copy.

Writing Mysteries

Follow the Clues

Samantha and Josh's whole class wrote mysteries. Read Josh's story starting on the next page. Then learn how to write your own mystery.

Student MODEL

The Case of the Missing Ring

The main character is named.

Once there was a scientist named Josh. He and his friend Ryan went to the library a lot.

In the library, there was a wooden sculpture. It had a shiny ring with a picture of a crow on it. Everyone thought the shiny ring was cool.

The mystery or problem is talked about.

One day Josh and Ryan met at the library. Ryan saw that the ring was gone. There were no scratches on the wood.

Ryan said, "Josh, come here."

Josh checked for fingerprints. "No fingerprints," he said to Ryan.

→

Then Josh heard a strange sound. He looked to his left and his right. Nothing was there.

Josh saw the library's birdcage. The cage door was open, and the pet crow was gone.

He remembered there were no scratches or fingerprints. He thought about the ring. "I have

solved the mystery," he thought.

Josh looked up. There was the crow. It had the ring in its beak!

Ryan said, "Maybe the crow thought the picture on the ring was real."

Josh said, "That's right. Maybe the crow needed a friend."

Case closed.

Steps in Writing a Mystery Story

1 **PLAN**

List Problems to Solve
Here are some ideas:
- a lost key
- a missing gerbil
- a noise in the attic

Choose One Problem

Plan Your Story

* Who will solve your problem?
* What other characters will be in your story?
* Where will it take place?

2 WRITE

Start Your Story

Try to do these things:

* Introduce your main character.

* Tell about the problem.

* Let your reader know why the mystery has *got* to be solved.

Keep It Going

Put in clues for the main character to follow.

Solve the Mystery

Add a finishing touch.

Josh wrote,
"Case closed."

If you get stuck, reread Josh's mystery. See how he put his story together.

3 REVISE

Read Your First Draft

Ask yourself two main questions:

Did I put in some clues?

Did I solve my mystery?

Make Changes

Be sure your mystery is exciting. Have your characters speak to each other.

GOOD POINT

Indent each time someone new speaks. It will make your story easier to read.

4 CHECK

Check for Errors

Check your sentences for capital letters, end punctuation, and spelling.

150

Poetry Writing

Writing Small Poems

The Pool

I live at the pool
in the summer.
The water is green
like a slice of kiwi.
I flip off the diving board—
SPLASH—
a belly flop.

Every Word Counts

"The Pool" is a small poem by Clay. Writing a small poem is a fun way to tell about everyday things. Clay says, "You can say neat things without using lots of words."

Another MODEL

The words in Ginna's poem show how
the beach looks and feels.

At the Beach

Waves are dark green
before the rain.
Saltwater feels warmest
after it rains.
Foamy waves look like bubbles
on root beer.
Maybe I will float and get near
big waves that will push me
onto the beach.
I'll reach. I'll reach.

by Ginna

Making Friends with Small Poems

Follow these tips when you read small poems.

READ the poem two or three times.

READ it aloud and listen to the sounds.

SHARE the poem with a partner.

COPY the poem into your notebook.

Which words help you see pictures?

Which words tell feelings?

Writing a Small Poem

1 PLAN

List Poem Ideas

Think of everyday things:

a toothbrush
the wind
stars
pebbles

Choose One Idea

Then list words and phrases about your idea. Anne listed words about the wind.

The wind

- feel it
- brushes my face
- blows seeds

2 WRITE — Write Your Poem

Here are some ideas to write about:

* Tell what your subject looks, smells, or sounds like.
* Tell what it does, or what you do with it.
* Tell how you feel about it.

Here are some special things to try:

* Use strong action words.

    I <u>flip</u> off the diving board—

* Make comparisons.

    The water is green
    like a slice of kiwi.

* Add sound to your poem. (Try repeating consonant sounds.)

    Foamy waves <u>l</u>ook <u>l</u>ike
    bub<u>b</u>les on root beer.

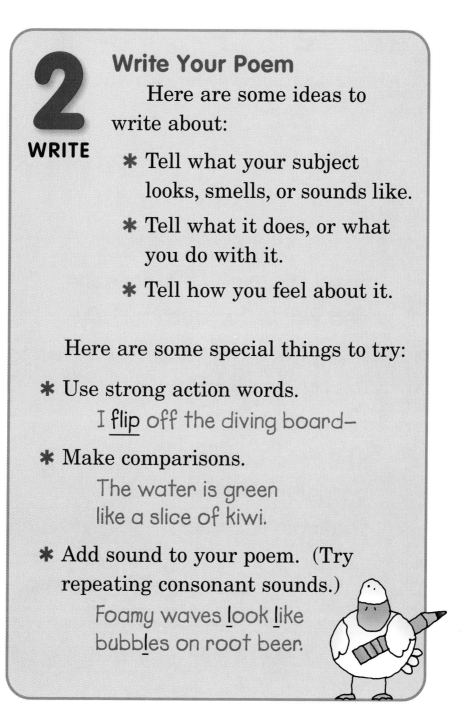

Anne's First Draft

Anne's draft shows she is trying to make her poem better.

The Wind

I feel the wind. It's ~~freezing~~ cold
and wants to brush my face.
I can't see the wind, ~~because~~
It's like an idea hidden
in my head.
The wind can blow
seeds and show
that rain is coming.

3 REVISE

Check Your First Draft

* Ask yourself questions:

   Have I used the best words?

   Have I made special comparisons?

* Mark where you want each line to end. Anne wanted to end her first line with the word "wind."

   I feel the wind./It's cold

4 CHECK

Check for Errors

✔ Check for spelling, capital letters, and punctuation.

✔ Then write your final copy. (See page 159 for Anne's final copy.)

Making Pleasing Sounds

Rhyme

Use rhyme to add sound to a poem.

Foamy waves look like
bubbles on root <u>beer</u>.
Maybe I will float and get <u>near</u>

Repeating Sounds

Try repeating words to add special sound to a poem.

I'll reach. I'll reach.

Or try repeating consonant sounds.

Waves a<u>r</u>e da<u>r</u>k g<u>r</u>een

Onomatopoeia

This term stands for words that make a sound. Use "sound words" in your poems.

<u>SPLASH</u>—
a belly flop.

Making Comparisons

- A **simile** makes a comparison using *like* or *as:*

      Shooting stars fall . . .
      <u>like</u> galloping horses.

- **Personification** makes a thing seem like a person:

      The wind wants to brush *my* face.

Anne's Final Copy

The Wind

I feel the wind.
It's cold
And wants to brush *my* face.
I can't see the wind.
It's like an idea
Hidden in *my* head.
The wind can blow seeds
And show that rain is coming.

Making Shape Poems

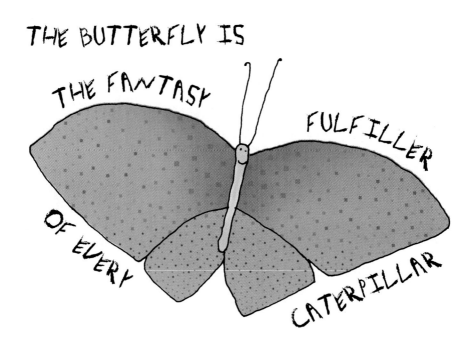

THE BUTTERFLY IS
THE FANTASY
FULFILLER
OF EVERY
CATERPILLAR

Do you like to doodle and draw?

J. Patrick Lewis does! So he makes shape poems like the butterfly above. You can, too. We will show you how.

MODEL

You can pour words *into* a shape to make a shape poem.

My
green balloon
is a toy airplane
without wings. It
floats like a bird in the
sky. A strong wind makes
me and my balloon run
fast and fall to the
ground. POP! The
balloon is pieces of
rubber drifting
to the grass.

Clarke

MODEL

You can also use words to *outline* a shape, as Jaime did.

White cotton balls float by, chased by wind that blows in the sky.

CLOUDS

Making a Shape Poem

1 PLAN

List Shapes

Think of things you like to play with or do.

> football
> kites
> swing
> blow bubbles

Choose a Shape

Make sure you can draw it.

Collect Ideas for Writing

Clarke thought about his shape, a balloon. Here are some ideas he collected.

> green
> floats
> a bird in the sky

2 WRITE

Write Your Poem
Circle your best ideas. Put the ideas together into a poem.

Draw Your Shape
Make it big enough for your words.

Put Your Poem and Shape Together
Write your poem either inside the shape or around it.

3 REVISE

Read Your First Draft

* **Ask yourself:** Do my ideas tell about my shape?
* **Ask a friend:** What do you see when you read my poem?

4 CHECK

Check for Errors

Check for spelling, capital letters, and punctuation. Then make a neat final copy of your poem to share.

Four More Poem Ideas

ABC Poem

An **ABC poem** uses parts of the
alphabet to make a funny list poem.

> All
> Bubbles
> Can
> Dance
> Easily

Diamond Poem

To write a **diamond poem**, follow a
syllable pattern. (Lines two and six name
the subject.)

Cold	(one syllable)
winter	(two syllables)
warm knit cap	(three syllables)
mittens, sweater	(four syllables)
long red scarf	(three syllables)
winter	(two syllables)
Fun	(one syllable)

Name Poetry

A **name poem** is made by using the letters of a name or a word to begin each line.

Cute	Sunny
Happy	Planting
Red hair	Rainy
Interesting	Insects
Silly	Nests
	Gardening

Tongue Twisters

The words in a **tongue twister** begin with the same letter or sound. Say the words really fast and feel your tongue twist!   Here are two examples:

Halloween
Crispy, Crunchy, Creamy, Candy

Nosey Nick
Nick knotted ninety-nine noses.

The TOOLS of Learning

Reading Skills

Reading Graphics

Some pictures are just fun to look at. Other pictures give information. Pictures that give information are called **graphics**.

Picture Perfect

This chapter will help you read four kinds of graphics: **signs, diagrams, tables,** and **bar graphs**.

Reading Signs

A **sign** tells something important.

This sign means "poison."

Mr. Yuk © Children's Hospital of Pittsburgh, PA.
Used with permission.

Clues for Understanding

- Look for letters or words on the sign.

  The RR on this sign stands for "railroad."

- Look for a slash. It means "no" or "not."

  This sign means "no bicycles."

- Look at the color of the sign.

  RED **may mean "stop" or "don't."**
  YELLOW **may mean "be careful."**
  GREEN **may mean "go here."**

Reading Diagrams

A **diagram** shows the parts of something or how something moves or changes.

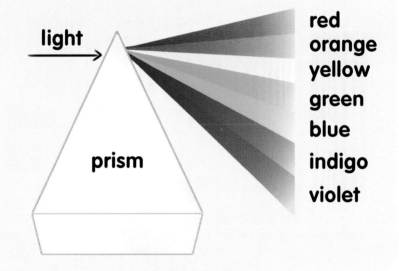

Light Moving Through a Prism

light

prism

red
orange
yellow
green
blue
indigo
violet

Clues for Understanding

- Look at the parts and then the whole diagram.
- Read the labels.
- Look at any arrows or pointer lines. They show how something moves or changes.

Reading Tables

A **table** is a good way to sort things.

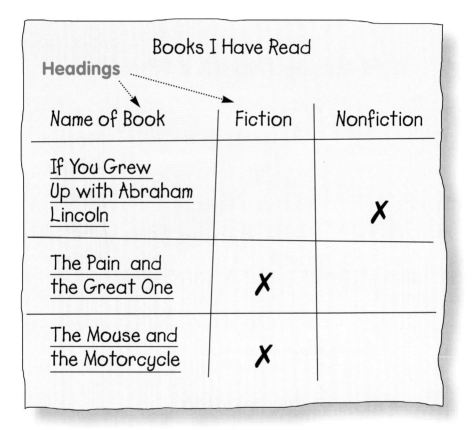

Books I Have Read

Headings

Name of Book	Fiction	Nonfiction
If You Grew Up with Abraham Lincoln		X
The Pain and the Great One	X	
The Mouse and the Motorcycle	X	

Clues for Understanding

- Read the title to see what the table is about.
- Read the headings.
- Read across each row.

Reading Bar Graphs

A **bar graph** helps you show how many.

Second Graders' Favorite Foods

Clues for Understanding

- Read the title to see what the table is about.
- Read the labels at the bottom of the bars.
- Read the scale at the side of the graph. It shows how many.

Reading
New Words

There are many ways to read new words. We show you some of them in this chapter.

LOOK for clues.

Read the whole sentence, but skip the word you don't know. Then think of a word that would make sense and sound right.

The **letters** in the word and the **pictures** and **ideas** on the page will help you.

LO⊙K for parts you know.

If you can read the word **cat**, you can read . . .

cattle   catch

If you can read **amp**, you can read . . .

camp   ramp   stamp

 Words like *camp* and *ramp* are in the same family. They have the same vowel and ending letters.

LO⊙K for sounds.

When you sound out a word, you try to say the word little by little.

To sound out "map," say . . .

/m/ /mă/ map

To sound out "bake," say . . .

/b/ /bā/ bake

LOOK for syllables.

Some words are too long to sound out!
You need to divide them into **syllables**.
Here are two ways to divide words:

Between double consonants

yel • low   ap • ple

Between two different consonants

pic • ture   sham • poo

LOOK for prefixes, suffixes, and root words.

Long words may include the root plus a
prefix, a suffix, or both.

		prefix	root	suffix
unpack	**=**	**un +**	**pack**	
dishes	**=**		**dish +**	**es**
returning	**=**	**re +**	**turn +**	**ing**

LOOK for compound words.

Big words may be made up of two smaller words. These big words are called **compound words**.

football = foot + ball

backpack = back + pack

grasshopper = grass + hopper

If you still can't read the word, ask for help.

Reading to Understand

Funny stories make you laugh. Special poems make you feel good. And interesting fact books make you a little smarter!

Planning to Learn

This chapter will help you read fact books. Each page lists a new plan that will help you read, learn, and remember.

Preview and Predict

Think about your reading before you start. Then you will be ready to learn! Here is a plan to follow:

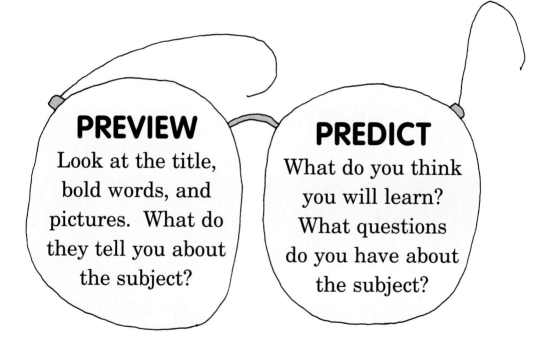

PREVIEW

Look at the title, bold words, and pictures. What do they tell you about the subject?

PREDICT

What do you think you will learn? What questions do you have about the subject?

Make sure to think about the subject *while* you read, and *after* you read. Did you find answers to your questions?

Know Want Learn

A KWL chart will help you think and learn when you read. Here is how to set up your chart:

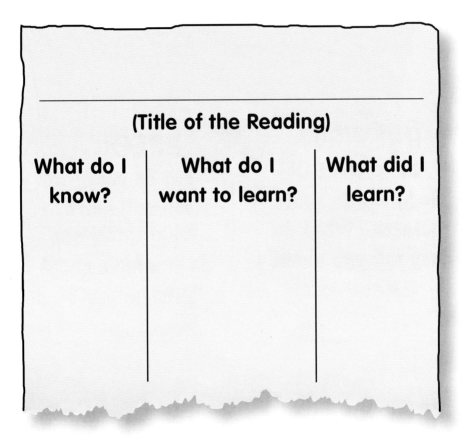

(Title of the Reading)

What do I know?	What do I want to learn?	What did I learn?

TIP Fill in the first two columns *before* you read. Fill in the last column *after* you read.

Retelling

Tell a classmate or your teacher about your reading. Talking, or retelling, helps show what you have learned. These questions will help you get started:

- What is the most important thing you learned?
- What other things did you learn?
- Are there pictures you'd like to show?

You can do your "retelling" on paper, too. Just write down all of the things you learned.

Mapping

Mapping, or clustering, helps you keep track of the main ideas in your reading. Here is a map for a book chapter about plants. (The name of the chapter is in the middle circle.)

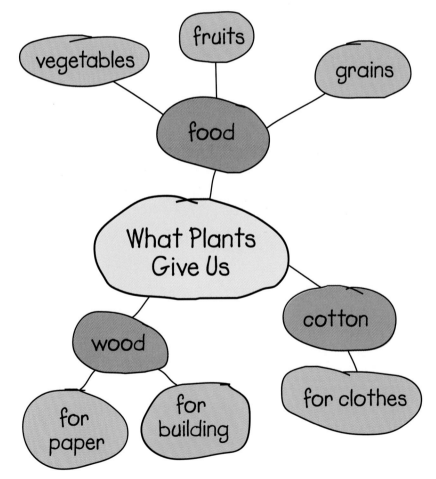

Drawing to Learn

Drawing pictures about your reading is a lot of fun. It also shows what you have learned! Sam read about animal houses. He drew pictures about this topic.

Working with Words

Using Phonics

Do you know your consonant and vowel sounds? They can help you learn new words in your reading. They can also help you spell words in your writing.

Sounding Out

This chapter is your guide to phonics. It gives examples of the basic consonant and vowel sounds. Check here when you need help with "sounding out."

Consonant Sounds

butterfly

cup cereal

duck

fish

girl gem

hat

jacket

kite

ladybug

mouse

nest

penguin

quilt

rocket

socks

turtle

vase

wagon

box

yarn

zipper

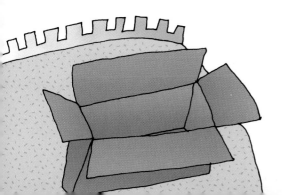

Using Consonant Blends

Consonant blends are two or more consonants that come together. Each letter keeps its own sound. Here are the basic consonant blends:

r blends **brush, cry, drip, frog grass, pretty, trip**

l blends **blue, cloud, flag glass, play, slide**

s blends **skip, smile, snap spot, star, swing scrap, spring, straw**

ending blends **band, pink, desk went, must**

Using Consonant Digraphs

Consonant digraphs are two consonant letters that come together and have one sound. Some basic consonant digraphs are:

ch chair, lunch, kitchen

gh enough, laughter

ph phone, elephant

sh shirt, dish, sunshine

th this, thin, bath

wh wheel, what

ng sing, rang, hanger

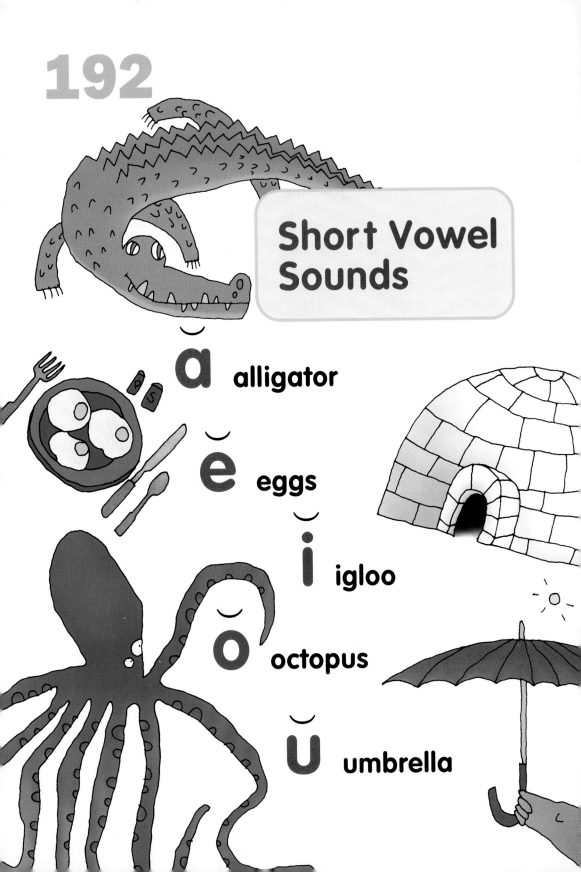

Short Vowel Sounds

ă alligator

ĕ eggs

ĭ igloo

ŏ octopus

ŭ umbrella

Using Short Vowels

Most words with short vowel sounds have this pattern:

consonant - vowel - consonant

short ă   cat   fat   bag

short ĕ   get   bed   men

short ĭ   pin   hill   big

short ŏ   hot   pop   fox

short ŭ   rug   duck   fun

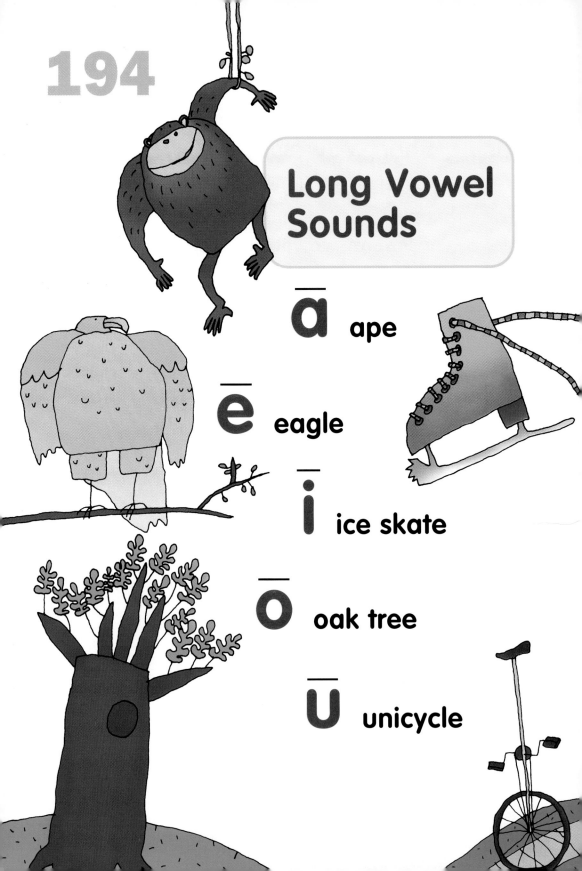

Long Vowel Sounds

ā ape

ē eagle

ī ice skate

ō oak tree

ū unicycle

Using Long Vowels

Words with long vowel sounds have many different patterns.

long ā   game   train   day

long ē   meat   street   Pete

long ī   time   pie   my   night

long ō   boat   hope   go

long ū   mule   suit   Sue

GOOD POINT

Sometimes "y" is a vowel, like at the end of "funn<u>y</u>" and "fl<u>y</u>."

Using R-Controlled Vowels

Vowels followed by the letter "r" have special sounds.

ar	barn, are, cart
or	fork, more, for
er	fern, person, letter
ir	bird, fir, girl
ur	curl, hurt, burn

The sounds of /er/, /ir/, and /ur/ are the same.

Using Diphthongs

Diphthongs (*say* `dif-thongs) are two vowel sounds that come together. They make a new sound.

oy/oi	toy, point, coin
ou/ow	out, round, cow
au/aw	haul, jaw, crawl
ew	stew, blew, drew

The same diphthong sound can have different spellings.

- You can hear /ew/ in **stew** and **cool**.

- You can hear /aw/ in words like **jaw, talk,** and **moth**.

Making New Words

The word "paint" is a root or base word. You can make "paint" into a new word by adding a word part.

A **prefix** is a part you add to the beginning of a root or base word.

re + paint = repaint

A **suffix** is a part you add to the end of a root or base word.

paint + ing = painting

Making New Words with Prefixes

The prefix **re** means "again."

re + build = rebuild

re + tell = retell

re + tie = retie

The prefix **un** means "not."

un + button = unbutton

un + happy = unhappy

un + sure = unsure

The prefix **tri** means "three."

tri + angle = triangle

tri + cycle = tricycle

tri + color = tricolor

Making New Words with Suffixes

The suffix **ed** means "past."

call + ed = called

play + ed = played

ski + ed = skied

The suffix **er** can mean "a person who does something."

farm + er = farmer

sing + er = singer

teach + er = teacher

The suffix **ing** means "doing or acting."

catch + ing = catching

read + ing = reading

walk + ing = walking

More Prefixes

bi (meaning "two")
bicycle (a two-wheeled vehicle)

ex (meaning "out")
exit (to go out)

sub (meaning "under")
submarine (an underwater ship)

More Suffixes

er (meaning "more")
slower (more slow)

est (meaning "most")
slowest (most slow)

ly (meaning "in some way")
slowly (in a slow way)

s, es (meaning "more than one, plural")
balloons (more than one balloon)
boxes (more than one box)

Making Contractions

A **contraction** is a shorter word made from one or two longer words. An apostrophe (') shows that one or more letters is left out.

Waldo doesn't stop playing.

He's a musical monkey!

cannot	can't	is not	isn't
could not	couldn't	it is	it's
did not	didn't	should not	shouldn't
do not	don't	they are	they're
does not	doesn't	was not	wasn't
has not	hasn't	we are	we're
have not	haven't	we have	we've
he is	he's	will not	won't
I am	I'm	would not	wouldn't
I have	I've	you are	you're
I will	I'll	you have	you've

Using a Glossary

A **glossary** is like a little dictionary in the back of a book. It tells about special words used in the book.

Here are some things you will find on a glossary page:

Guide Words: These are the words at the top of a page. They tell you where you are in the alphabet.

Spelling: The glossary shows the correct spelling of each word.

Meaning: The meaning helps you understand the word.

Sentence: The word is used in a sentence to make the meaning very clear.

MODEL

guide word *Glossary* guide word

above **began**

A

above in a higher place (The stars were shining *above*.)

already by this time (By ten o'clock, you should *already* be at school.)

angry mad; feeling anger (Molly was *angry* when she couldn't find her crayons.)
angrier, angriest

around on all sides of (In a toy shop, there are many toys *around* you.)

attic a room at the top of some houses, just under the roof (My family puts the things we don't use in the *attic*.)

B

backward with the back end first (The car moved *backward* down the road.)

bandage a strip of cloth or paper that you put over a place on your body that has been hurt (When I cut my finger, Mom puts a *bandage* on it.)

beautiful very pretty (My new dress is *beautiful*.)

beaver an animal with brown fur and a wide tail that lives on land and in the water (The *beaver* cut down a tree with its teeth.)

because for a reason (I am afraid *because* it is dark here.)

began See **begin**.

Speaking and Listening Skills

Learning to View

Most of the time, you watch TV for fun. But programs like **TV specials** help you learn things, too.

Special Shows

TV specials can be about the rain forest, dinosaurs, or almost anything. This chapter gives you a plan for watching TV specials. You will also learn about other programs and commercials.

Wild Animals

Watching to Learn

Before the Special

- **List** questions you have about the subject.

  What is a dinosaur?

  How many dinosaurs were there?

  How do we know about them?

During the Special

- **Look** for answers to your questions.
- **Write** down key words to help you remember.

  What is a dinosaur?
  - a reptile

  How many dinosaurs were there?
  - more than 800 kinds

  How do we know about them?
  - experts find fossils

After the Special

Here are some things you can do after the program:

- **Think** about your questions. Did you find answers to them?
- **Talk** about the special with someone.
- **Write** about the important ideas.

Dinosaurs

Dinosaurs were reptiles. You can tell dinosaurs by the special way they walked. Their bodies didn't drag on the ground. There were more than 800 kinds of dinosaurs. . . .

Talking and writing help you remember things!

Learning About TV Programs

There are two main types of TV programs. Some programs give **real** reports or show real events. Most other programs are **made-up** stories.

Shows like *Sesame Street* and *Carmen Sandiego* have some real parts and some made-up parts.

Learning About Commercials

Most **commercials** ask you to buy a product. They use bright colors and catchy words to make the product look and sound good. Here are some other things they do:

Using Famous People

Some commercials show a sports star using a product. If Shaq drinks _____ , it must be good! (Is this always true?)

Bandwagon

A commercial may show many kids eating a new candy bar. You may want to join the group and eat one, too!

Problem Solving

Some commercials show how a product solves a problem. Maybe new soccer shoes help a player do better. So they must be good! (Is this always true?)

Learning to Listen

Ears can be a problem. They collect dirt, and they get full of wax! But ears do a lot of good things, too. For example, they help keep your hat on top of your head. And they allow you to listen.

Tuning In

Listening is a great way to learn. You listen to your parents, your teachers, and your friends. The next page will show you how to be a good listener.

How to Be a Good Listener

Look at the person who is speaking. This will help you follow the speaker.

Listen for key words. They help you remember important facts.

> **The Pacific Ocean is the biggest ocean.**
>
> **The Arctic Ocean is the smallest ocean.**

Listen for directions. They tell you what to do.

> **Read about oceans on page 17.**
> **List new words you find.**

Ask questions. When you don't understand something, ask for help.

Learning to Interview

Interviewing is a fun way to learn. In an **interview**, you ask someone questions. The other person answers them. This chapter will show you how to interview.

Talking with a Doctor

Cheryl interviewed Jennifer Miller. Dr. Miller is a vet (animal doctor) who is deaf. At the end of this chapter, you will see what Cheryl learned.

Before the Interview

- **Write** questions to ask the person. Think of questions that begin with **why**, **how**, and **what**.

  Why did you become a vet?

  How did you learn in school?

- **Set up** a time and place to meet for the interview.

- **Gather** your supplies. You need your list of questions and two sharp pencils.

During the Interview

- **Introduce** yourself.
- **Ask** your questions one at a time.
- **Listen** carefully to the answers.
- **Take** notes.

Why did you become a vet?

— always loved animals

— played with stuffed animals

How did you learn in school?

- At the end, **thank** the person for the interview.

Thank you.

After the Interview

- **Share** what you have learned.

Here is Cheryl's report from her interview.

My Interview

Jennifer Miller is a veterinarian. She is also deaf.

Dr. Miller always loved animals. When she was little, she played with stuffed animals. It was hard for Dr. Miller to learn in school. Sometimes friends took notes for her.

Are you wondering how Dr. Miller answered my questions? She can read lips. She can also talk. I really liked interviewing Dr. Miller.

Performing Stories

Have you ever wanted to perform a story? That's just what Kasey and her friends did. They read one of her stories in a reader's theater performance.

Reader's Theater

In reader's theater, you don't have to learn the lines by heart. You read them! This chapter will show you how to plan and perform a story in this special way.

Planning to Perform

 Pick a Story ● Choose a story with characters who talk to each other a lot.

 Form a Team ● You will need a reader for each character. You will also need a narrator to read the nonspeaking parts.

 Mark the Speaking Parts ● Mark what each character and the narrator will say. You could also write the story in script form. (See the next two pages for help.)

 Practice Your Reading
● Decide who gets which part.
● Plan where to sit or stand.
● Practice the reading.

MODEL Story

Here is the first part of Kasey's story. On the next page, you will see her script.

The Yellow Elephant: Part 1

Once upon a time, Elmer went fishing by himself. His mom and dad said, "Don't talk to yellow elephants."

Elmer said, "OK!"

He went to his best fishing spot. He was so excited because he caught 10 fish. Then it was time to go home. On the way, he saw a yellow elephant.

The elephant said, "Hello!"

Elmer said, "My mom and dad told me not to talk to yellow elephants!"

"But I'm lost," said the elephant.

Elmer said, "OK, I will take you to my house."

"Oh, good!" said the yellow elephant.

"Now come on," said Elmer. And off they went.

MODEL Script

The Yellow Elephant: Part 1

NARRATOR: Once upon a time, Elmer went fishing by himself.

MOM AND DAD: Don't talk to yellow elephants, Elmer.

ELMER: OK, I won't.

NARRATOR: Elmer went to his best fishing spot. He was so excited because he caught 10 fish. Then it was time to go home. On the way, he saw a yellow elephant.

ELEPHANT: Hello!

ELMER: My mom and dad told me not to talk to yellow elephants!

ELEPHANT: But I'm lost.

ELMER: OK, I'll take you to my house. Come on.

ELEPHANT: Oh, good!

NARRATOR: So off they went.

To make a script, you may have to drop or change some words in the story.

Performing TIPS

Follow these tips when you are ready to perform your story:

INTRODUCE the story.

LOOK up from time to time when reading.

- Characters should look at the person they are talking to.
- The narrator should look at the audience.

USE your best outside voice.

KEEP going if someone makes a mistake.

JOIN hands and bow together at the end of the performance.

Important: Costumes are okay, as long as you keep them simple.

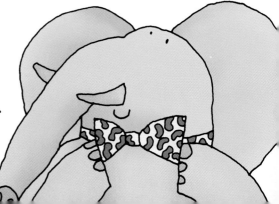

Next Step

Here is the second part of Kasey's story. Try writing a script for this part. Then practice and perform the whole story!

The Yellow Elephant: Part 2

"Mom! Dad!" yelled Elmer. "I have a yellow elephant!"

His mom and dad said, "Take him back where he was. He is dangerous."

"No, he isn't," said Elmer.

"Take him back," said his mom and dad.

Elmer took him back. By the time he got home, it was time to go to bed.

In the morning, he heard something. He looked outside. There was a yellow bird in a cage. He went outside and got it.

The bird whispered to him, "I am the yellow elephant," and Elmer believed him.

He asked his mom and dad if he could keep the bird, and they said, "Yes."

So he hung the cage up in his room, and they've kept it a secret ever since.

Telling Stories

Sometimes we hear a story that is so good, we want to tell it to our friends. Folktales can be like that. So can fairy tales and legends.

Once Upon a Time . . .

This chapter will help you tell stories. First you will read a folktale. (You can use this story for practice.) Then you will learn about some great storytelling tips.

MODEL Story

The Three Billy Goats Gruff

Once upon a time, there were three billy goats named Gruff. They wanted to go up to the hillside to eat, but they had to cross a bridge to get there. Under this bridge, lived a great, ugly troll.

The youngest Billy Goat Gruff was the first to cross the bridge. *Trip, trap! Trip, trap! Trip, trap!*

"Who's that trip-trapping over my bridge?" yelled the troll.

"It is I, the youngest Billy Goat Gruff. I am going up to the hillside to eat," said the scared little billy goat.

"Well, I'm going to gobble you up!" said the troll.

"Don't eat *me*. I'm too little," said the billy goat. "Wait for the second Billy Goat Gruff. He's bigger."

"Very well," said the troll.

Then the second Billy Goat Gruff walked across the bridge. *Trip, trap! Trip, trap! Trip, trap!*

"Who's that trip-trapping over my bridge?" yelled the troll.

"It is I, the second Billy Goat Gruff. I am going up to the hillside to eat."

$\rightarrow$

"Well, I'm going to gobble you up!" said the troll.

"Don't eat *me.* I'm not big enough," said the billy goat. "Wait for the oldest Billy Goat Gruff. He's much bigger."

"Very well," said the troll.

Just then the oldest Billy Goat Gruff walked across the bridge. *Trip, trap! Trip, trap! Trip, trap! Trip, trap!* He was very, very big.

"Who's that trip-trapping over my bridge?" yelled the troll.

"It is I, the oldest Billy Goat Gruff!" said the brave billy goat in a loud voice.

"Well, I'm going to gobble you up!" yelled the troll.

"Well, come along then! And I'll crush you to bits!" said the big Billy Goat Gruff.

Up rushed the troll, and the big Billy Goat Gruff took care of him in no time! After that, the oldest billy goat went up to the hillside with his brothers.

There the three billy goats got so fat, they were hardly able to walk home again.

So . . . snip, snap, snout, this tale's told out.

Storytelling TIPS

CHOOSE a story you really like—one that is not too long.

WRITE down the first and the last lines on different note cards. (Half sheets of paper work, too.) This way, you can read the beginning and the ending if you want to.

PRACTICE telling your story. Picture it in your head as you go along.

MAKE more note cards if you need them. Write down short clues to help you remember the main story parts.

USE your best voice. Add special feeling to important lines. (Don't talk too fast.)

TELL your story to your classmates or your family.

Giving Oral Reports

Do you have a collection? Do you know how to make something? Have you just read about an interesting subject?

Telling and Showing

You can share your special information in an oral report. An **oral report** is part telling and part showing. You tell important facts about your subject. And you show pictures or examples to go with the facts.

Planning Your Report

In the **beginning** . . .

- Name your subject in an interesting way.

In the **middle** . . .

- Give some main facts about your subject.
- Have pictures, charts, or examples to show.

In the **end** . . .

- Tell why this subject is important for you, or for others.

To help you remember things, list your main ideas on note cards.

Giving Your Report

- **Use** your best outside voice. (Don't speak too fast!)
- **Look** at your classmates.
- **Try** to stand still.

Learning Skills

Getting Organized

To play a board game, you have to get organized. You must get out all the pieces, and set them up in the right way.

Thinking on Paper

When you think about an important subject, you have to get organized, too. This chapter will show you how.

Clustering

A **cluster** helps you remember details about a subject. Write your subject in the middle of your paper. Circle it. Then write the details around your subject.

Clustering helps you remember details for all-about-me stories.

Describing a Subject

A **describing wheel** helps you describe a subject. Write your subject in the middle of the wheel. Write your describing words on the spokes.

Describing words can be things you see, hear, feel, smell, or taste.

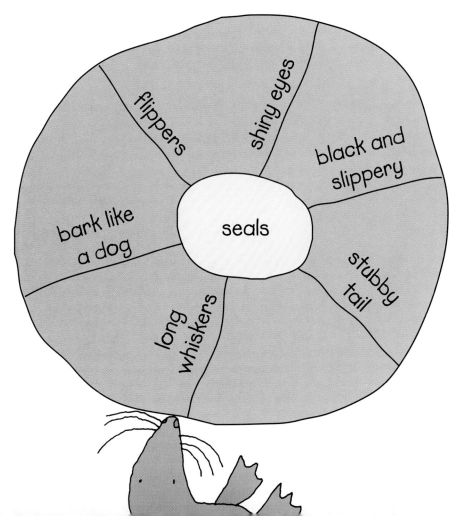

Comparing Two Subjects

A **Venn diagram** helps you compare two subjects. It has three spaces to fill in.

In spaces 1 and 2, you show how two subjects are different. In space 3, you show how the subjects are alike.

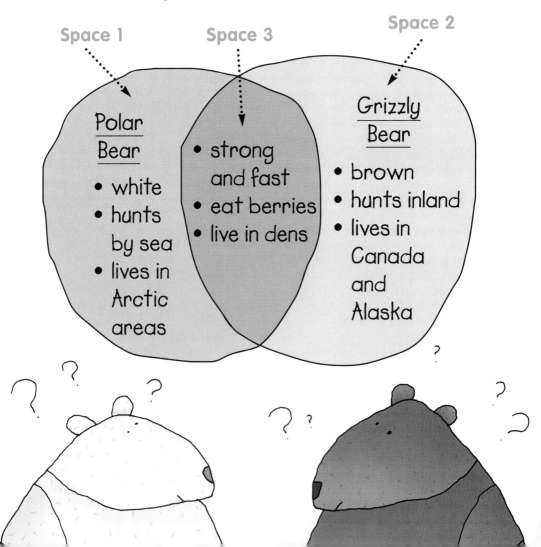

Space 1   Space 3   Space 2

Polar
Bear
• white
• hunts
by sea
• lives in
Arctic
areas

• strong
and fast
• eat berries
• live in dens

Grizzly
Bear
• brown
• hunts inland
• lives in
Canada
and
Alaska

Making a Story Map

A **story map** helps you remember the important parts in a story. You can write words or draw pictures for the parts of a story.

Jack and the Beanstalk

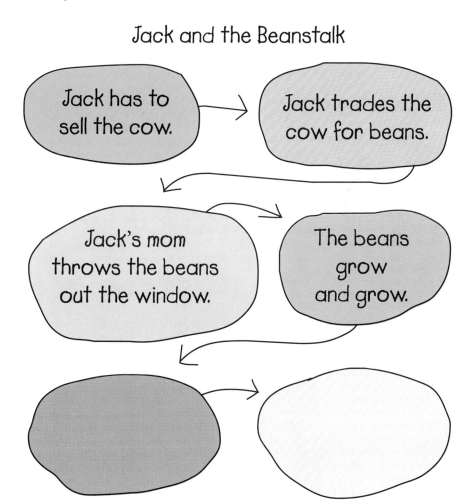

Working in Groups

Everybody works in groups. Doctors and firefighters work in groups. So do cookie bakers and second graders!

Teaming Up

Why do we work in groups? Groups help us finish big jobs. What must everybody in a group remember to do? Everybody must get along and try hard.

Planning TIPS

TALK about your assignment or job. Make sure everybody understands it.

SHARE your ideas. Take turns and listen carefully.

PLAN the work. Everybody should have a job to do.

PUT your plan on paper.

Group Plan

1. Our job is to ___plan a welcome party___ .

2. Our due date is ___Friday___ .

3. Things we need to do:

   - Vijay and Tonya will bring cookies.
   - Steve and Marcie will make a banner.
   - Tonya will write a welcome speech.

Taking Tests

School keeps you busy. You read and write. You practice new skills. You make things. And you take tests!

Learning and Showing

Tests are not as much fun as some of the things you do. But they are important. This chapter will help you become a good test taker.

D. Adjectives   Name _Tommy Sims_

_100%_

Fill in the circle before the word that best completes each sentence.

1. Of the three bikes, this one is the _____.
   (A) most fastest
   (B) faster
   (C) more faster
   ● fastest

2. A truck is _____ than a car.
   (A) big
   (B) m____
   ● ____er
   (D) ____ big

3. _____uters are the _____ machines of all.
   smarter
   (B) most smartest
   ● smartest
   (D) more smarter

Great Job, Tommy!

Matching Test

A **matching** test gives two lists of words. You must find the words from each list that go together.

- Study both lists very carefully.

- Then start with the first word in the left column. Try it with each word in the right column until you make a match.

Example:

MAKING COMPOUND WORDS

Directions: Draw a line between the words in both lists that go together.

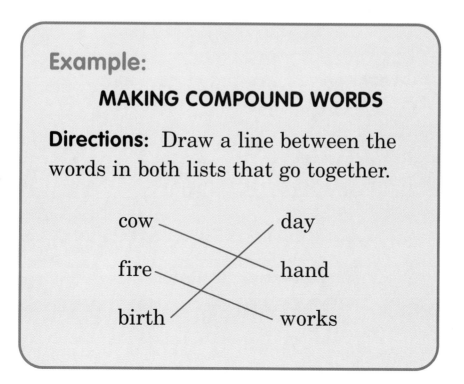

Multiple-Choice Test

A **multiple-choice** test gives a list of sentences to complete. You must pick the best choice to complete each sentence.

- Read the sentence with each choice.
- Then reread the sentence with your best choice. Be sure it makes sense.

Example:

FARM ANIMALS

Directions: Fill in the circle before the word that best completes each sentence.

1. A baby sheep is called a _____.

   (a) calf   (b) lamb   (c) fawn

2. A group of sheep is called a _____.

   (a) fawn   (b) band   (c) flock

Fill-in-the-Blank Test

A **fill-in-the-blank** test gives a list of sentences to complete. You must write the correct word or words in the blanks.

- Read each sentence very carefully.
- Count how many blanks you need to fill.
- Be sure your answer makes sense.

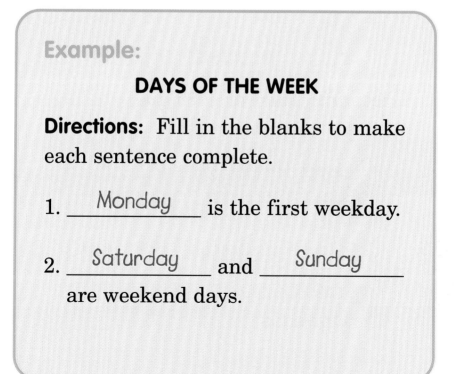

Example:

DAYS OF THE WEEK

Directions: Fill in the blanks to make each sentence complete.

1. ____Monday____ is the first weekday.

2. ____Saturday____ and ____Sunday____ are weekend days.

Short-Answer Test

A **short-answer** test gives you questions to answer in sentences.

- Read the question.
- Think about your answer.
- Write your sentence. Use a few words from the question in your sentence.

Example:

WEATHER

Directions: Answer each question in a complete sentence.

1. What are clouds made of?
   Clouds are made of tiny drops of water.

2. What is a blizzard?
   A blizzard is a snowstorm with strong winds.

Test-Taking **TIPS**

WRITE your name on your paper.

FOLLOW along as your teacher goes over the directions.

ASK questions if you do not understand something.

ANSWER the questions you know.

SKIP over the ones you're not sure of.

Then **GO BACK** to the unanswered questions.

> Check to make sure you answered all the questions.

The Proofreader's GUIDE

The Proofreader's Guide

Using Punctuation

A "walk" signal tells us to go. A "don't walk" signal tells us to stop. These signals are very important.

Stopping and Going

Punctuation marks are signals we use in writing. For example, we use a period to signal a stop at the end of a sentence. You can learn about using punctuation in this chapter.

When to Use a Period

At the End of a Telling Sentence

George and Martha are silly.

After an Abbreviation

Mr. Plant

Ms. Blossom

Dr. Weed

Between Dollars and Cents

I have $2.25 in my pocket.

When to Use a Question Mark

After a Question

Who sat on my lunch?

When to Use an Exclamation Point

After an "Excited" Word

Wow!   Awesome!   Yuck!

After a Sentence Showing Strong Feelings

There's a skunk on the playground!

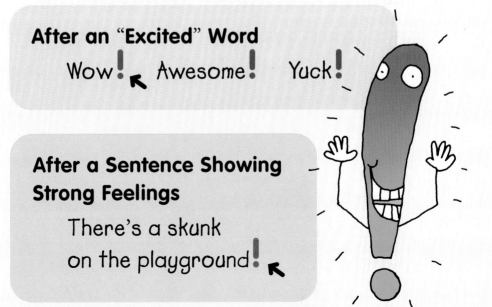

When to Use a Comma

**Between a City
and a State**
El Paso, Texas

**Between the Day
and the Year**
July 4, 1776

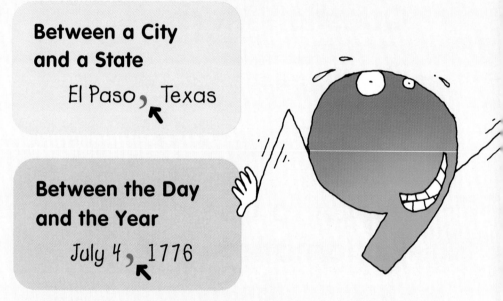

After the Greeting in a Letter
Dear Grandpa,

After the Closing in a Letter
Love,
Liz

Between Words in a Series

I love red, purple, and silver.

To Keep Big Numbers Clear

My big brother is trying to save $10,000!

To Help Set Off a Speaker's Words

Ross said, "I love kickball!"

A comma looks like a period with a tail on it (,).

When to Use an Apostrophe

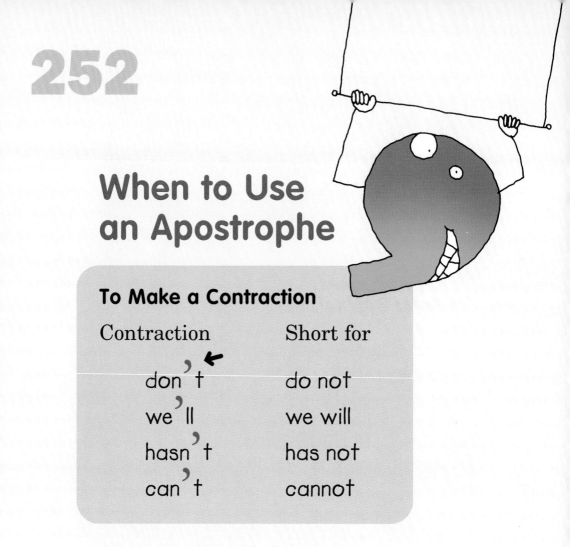

To Make a Contraction

Contraction	Short for
don't	do not
we'll	we will
hasn't	has not
can't	cannot

To Show That Someone Owns Something

my brother's frog
(One person owns the frog.)

the teachers' cars
(Two or more people own cars.)

When to Use Quotation Marks

Before and After a Speaker's Words

"I love carrots," said Sam.

For Titles of Stories and Poems

I called my story "Our New Pet."

When to Use Underlining

For Titles of Books and Magazines

I just read Arthur's Halloween.

Checking Mechanics

Rules help us in many ways. We have rules that help us keep safe. We have rules that help us play games. We also have rules that help us with our writing.

Rules for Writing

This chapter lists rules for the **mechanics of writing**. (*Say* mi-`kan-iks.) You will learn about using capital letters, writing plurals, and much more. *Remember:* Rules help us write!

Using Capital Letters

For the First Word in a Sentence
↗ Fireflies light up the garden.

For a Speaker's First Word
Mr. Smith said, "Look at this
spiderweb." ↗

For Names and Titles
→ Jackie Wilson
↘ Dr. Small

For the Word "I"
What will I say to him?
↗

Using Capital Letters

For Titles of Books, Stories, Poems, . . .

→ <u>Arthur's Halloween</u> (book)

"Lost in the Woods" (story)

"Elephant for Sale" (poem)

<u>Spider</u> (magazine)

For Days, Months, and Holidays

→ Friday   January   Thanksgiving

For Names of Places

→ Canada   Rocky Mountains

Ohio   Main Street

Chicago   Sears Tower

Making Plurals

Add "**s**" to make the plural of most nouns.

bug – bug**s** wing – wing**s**

Add "**es**" to make the plural of nouns ending in *s, x, sh,* and *ch.*

glass – glass**es** bush – bush**es**

Change the word to make the plural of some nouns.

child – **children** man – **men**

Change the "y" to "i" and add "es" to nouns with a consonant before the *y.*

sky – sk**ies** story – stor**ies**

Using Abbreviations

For Titles of People

→ Mr.   Ms.   Mrs.   Dr.

For Addresses on Envelopes

MS JOAN CAPEWELL
FIRST NATIONAL BANK
101 MAIN ST
MILWAUKEE WI 50100

(The post office says to use capital letters and no punctuation on envelopes.)

Post Office Address Abbreviations

Avenue	AVE	North	N
Boulevard	BLVD	Road	RD
Court	CT	South	S
Drive	DR	Square	SQ
East	E	Street	ST
Highway	HWY	West	W

Post Office State Abbreviations

Alabama	AL	Montana	MT
Alaska	AK	Nebraska	NE
Arizona	AZ	Nevada	NV
Arkansas	AR	New Hampshire	NH
California	CA	New Jersey	NJ
Colorado	CO	New Mexico	NM
Connecticut	CT	New York	NY
Delaware	DE	North Carolina	NC
District of Columbia	DC	North Dakota	ND
Florida	FL	Ohio	OH
Georgia	GA	Oklahoma	OK
Hawaii	HI	Oregon	OR
Idaho	ID	Pennsylvania	PA
Illinois	IL	Rhode Island	RI
Indiana	IN	South Carolina	SC
Iowa	IA	South Dakota	SD
Kansas	KS	Tennessee	TN
Kentucky	KY	Texas	TX
Louisiana	LA	Utah	UT
Maine	ME	Vermont	VT
Maryland	MD	Virginia	VA
Massachusetts	MA	Washington	WA
Michigan	MI	West Virginia	WV
Minnesota	MN	Wisconsin	WI
Mississippi	MS	Wyoming	WY
Missouri	MO		

Checking Your Spelling

This spelling list includes many of the important words you will use in your writing. Check this list when you are not sure how to spell a word. (Also check a classroom dictionary for help.)

A

about
again
alone
animal
ant
are
ask
aunt
away

B

back
bad
bank
bed
been
before
believe
bell
best
big
black
blocks
blue
boat
bones
book
born
box
bricks
bright
broke

broom
brother
brown
burn
but
by

C

cake
call
candle
candy
cards
chicken
chicks
children
clean
clock
colors
comes
cookies
corner

could
crowded

D

daddy
dance
dark
desks
didn't
doesn't
dog
doll
dollars
done
don't
door
dream
drop
dropping
duck

E

each
eat
eggs
eight
eye

F

fall
farm
fast
feather
feel
fight
fire
five
floor
flowers
fly
flying

food
foot
for
forgot
fort
four
Friday
frog
front
full
fun
funny

G

game
give
going
good
grass
green

H

hair
half
hall
hand
happen
hard
has
head
help
hid
hidden
high
hill
hit
hook
hope
horse
hot
hours
how
hurt

I

I
ice
I'm
its
it's
I've

J

jam
jelly
just

K

keep
kids
kite
kitten
knew

L

lady
land
last
laugh
let
letter
licked
light
log
lonely
look
lot
loud
love

M

make
many
may
men

milk
Monday
money
monkey
month
moon
more
morning
most
mouse
move

N

name
need
new
next
nice
night
nine
not
now

O

okay
once
one
open
orange
other
ours

P

party
penny
play
please
poor
porch
post
pour
pretty
pull
purple

Q

quick
quiet

R

rabbit
rain
ready
really
ride
road
rode
room
rope

S

said
Saturday
says
school
seven
shoes
should
six
skies
sleep
socks
soft
something
soon
sound
stairs
stick
still
stopping
store
storm
street
summer
Sunday
sure
swimming
swing

T

take
teacher
teeth
tell
ten
thank
their
there
they're
three
Thursday
told
tooth
train
tree
trucks
try
Tuesday
turkeys
turn
two

U

under
until
use

V

van
very

W

wall
water
weather
Wednesday
week
went
what
when
where
white

who
why
wish
women
won
wool
work
would

X

X ray

Y

year
yellow
your
you're

Z

zoo

Spelling **TIPS**

Make a SPELLING NOTEBOOK

Save one or two pages for each letter in the alphabet. Write **A** at the top of the "**A word**" pages, **B** at the top of the "**B word**" pages, and so on. When you find words that are hard, add them to your notebook.

Read over your notebook often. You will soon know how to spell the words.

Use a SPELLING PLAN

Use a plan to practice a new word:

* Look at the word and say it.
* Spell it aloud.
* Cover the word and spell it on paper.
* Check the spelling.
* If you made a mistake, try again.

Learn Some
SPELLING TRICKS

For some words, you may make the same mistake over and over again. When this happens, try one of these tricks:

* Say the word aloud. Say the hard letters the loudest.

  Say rabbit like **rabBIT**.

* Spell the word on paper. Underline the hard letters, or print them bigger than the other letters.

* Think of a saying to help you remember a spelling:

  A bear is hidDEN in the DEN.

Using the Right Word

Some words sound alike, but they have different spellings. They also have different meanings. These words are called **homophones**.

ant   An **ant** crawled onto my finger.

aunt   My **aunt** likes to tell jokes.

ate   Liz **ate** lunch with me.

eight   I have **eight** crayons.

bare   My bare hands are freezing.

bear   Ira has a teddy bear.

blew   Dakota blew the biggest bubble.

blue   A robin's egg is blue.

dear   My grandma is a dear woman.

deer   The deer ran into the woods.

eye   Lu winks her eye.

I   I love to draw cats.

for   Miss Nelson made cookies for us.

four   Nick ate four tacos.

hear — I like to hear birds sing.

here — Who sits here?

knew — I knew my ABC's last year.

new — We have a new girl in our class.

know — Do you know her name?

no — Robert said, "No, I don't."

made — We made popcorn for a snack.

maid — Amelia Bedelia is a funny maid.

meat — Some people don't eat meat.

meet — I'll meet you at the clubhouse.

one My baby brother is **one** year old.

won Liz **won** a prize at the fair.

read Mr. Lee **read** a funny poem.

red I gave him a **red** apple.

road Tony lives on a country **road**.

rode He **rode** his bike to school.

sea A **sea** is a big body of water.

see Come and **see** my pet snake.

Visitors Welcome

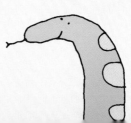

sew   My grandma likes to **sew** for me.

so   I'll hurry **so** we're not late.

son   My dad is the **son** of his dad.

sun   Plants need **sun** and water.

tail   A beaver has a flat **tail**.

tale   <u>Cinderella</u> is a fairy **tale**.

their   We used **their** bikes.
(*Their* shows ownership.)

there   **There** are four of them.

they're   **They're** mountain bikes.
(*they're* = they are)

to   I like **to** read funny books.

two   I read **two** joke books today.

too   Joe likes joke books, **too**.

wear   I like to **wear** floppy hats.

where   **Where** are you going?

wood   The fence is made of **wood**.

would   Dawn **would** like to go home.

your   What is **your** favorite video?

you're   **You're** a great singer.
(you're = you are)

Checking Your Sentences

What do I need to know?

A **sentence** tells a complete idea and has two parts.

1. The subject is the naming part.
2. The verb tells what the subject is doing.

My <u>**mom**</u> <u>**drives**</u> a motorbike.
  subject **verb**

A **sentence** begins with a capital letter. It ends with a period, a question mark, or an exclamation point.

→ Grandpa climbs trees. ←

Kinds of Sentences

A **telling sentence** (*declarative*) makes a statement.

> **Soccer is my favorite game.**

An **asking sentence** (*interrogative*) asks a question.

> **Will you play with me?**

A **directing sentence** (*imperative*) gives directions or a command.

> **Kick with the side of your foot.**

An **exclamatory sentence** shows strong feelings.

> **Watch out for the ball!**

Understanding Our Language

All of the words we use fit into eight groups. These groups are called the **parts of speech**.

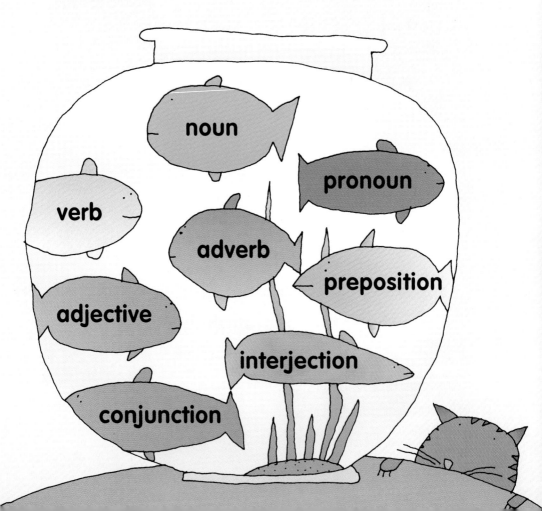

What is a noun?

A **noun** names a person, place, or thing.

girl   house   bike

Nouns can be **singular** or **plural**.

singular: neighbor   house

plural: neighbors   houses

Nouns can be **common** or **proper**.

common: boy   street

proper: Gus   Oak Street

A **possessive noun** shows ownership.

Julie's flute

the **boys'** tubas

What is a pronoun?

A **pronoun** is a word that takes the place of a noun. Here are some pronouns.

I	me	my	he
him	his	she	her
you	your	it	its
we	us	our	they
them	their		

How are pronouns used?

Pronouns stand for nouns in sentences.

Holly played a game.
She hid the penny.
(*She* is a pronoun.)

Erik made cookies.
Then **he** ate **them**.
(*He* and *them* are pronouns.)

What is a verb?

A **verb** shows action or helps complete a thought or an idea.

Spot **barks** at my neighbor.
Mr. Wilson **is** so mad!

Some verbs tell what is happening now, or in the **present**.

George **slips** on the banana peel.

Some verbs tell what happened in the **past**.

Sarah **walked** her dog.

Some verbs tell what will happen in the **future**.

I **will find** some shells.

What are the different forms of verbs?

Many verbs are **regular**.
You can add *ed* to them.

> I **laugh**.
> I **laughed**.
> I **have laughed**.
> (with helping word)

Some verbs are **irregular**. You usually can't add *ed* to them. They change in different ways.

> I **eat**.
> I **ate**.
> I **have eaten**.
> (with helping word)

TIP There is a list of irregular verbs on the next page.

Common Irregular Verbs

Present	Past	With Helping Word
am, is, are	was, were	been
begin	began	begun
break	broke	broken
catch	caught	caught
come	came	come
do	did	done
draw	drew	drawn
eat	ate	eaten
fall	fell	fallen
give	gave	given
go	went	gone
hide	hid	hidden, hid
know	knew	known
ride	rode	ridden
ring	rang	rung
run	ran	run
see	saw	seen
sing	sang, sung	sung
take	took	taken
throw	threw	thrown
write	wrote	written

What is an adjective?

An **adjective** describes a noun or pronoun.

> **Many** animals live in the jungle.
> An anaconda is a **giant** snake!

An **adjective** sometimes compares *two* nouns (or pronouns).

> An ant is **smaller** than an anaconda.

An adjective sometimes compares *more than two* nouns.

> An anteater is the **oddest** animal.

The words *a, an,* and *the* are **articles**.
Use *a* before a consonant sound:

> **a** parrot

Use *an* before a vowel sound:

> **an** otter

What are the other parts of speech?

An **adverb** is a word that describes a verb.

Erin ran **quickly**.   She fell **down**.

A **preposition** is used to help make a statement.

Maya laughed **at** the joke.

Joe sat **on** the beach.

A **conjunction** connects words or ideas.

I will dance **or** sing.

First I cried **and** then I laughed.

An **interjection** shows excitement.

Wow! Did you see that bug?

Yuck! I hate creepy crawlers!

Using Theme Words

DAYS/MONTHS

Sunday   Monday

Tuesday   Wednesday

Thursday   Friday   Saturday

January   February

March   April   May

June   July   August

September   October

November   December

SEASON/WEATHER WORDS

winter spring summer fall

sun sunny wind windy

breeze breezy degrees

rain snow sleet fog

cold hot lightning

storm tornado

hurricane clouds

thermometer

thunder warm

temperature hail

FOOD WORDS

apples   oranges   bananas

grapes   lettuce   peaches

strawberries   broccoli   potatoes

corn   carrots   bread   beans

peanut butter   spaghetti

jelly   pizza   cookies

cupcakes   milk   yogurt

ice cream   hamburgers   rice

hot dogs   chicken   cereal

sandwiches   muffins

COMMUNITY WORDS

apartment　　town　　city

house　　police officer　　doctor

mail carrier　　shopping mall

drugstore　　post office　　church

neighbor　　store　　firefighter

street　　movie theater　　school

plumber　　teacher　　grocery store

hospital　　librarian　　nurse

neighborhood　　gas station

garbage collector

The Student ALMANAC

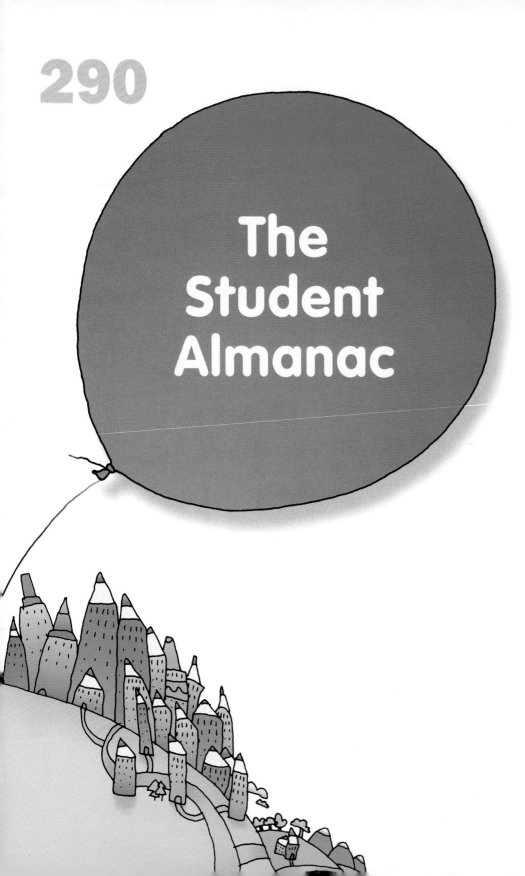

The Student Almanac

Useful Tables and Lists

The tables and lists in this section are interesting and fun to use.

Sign Language

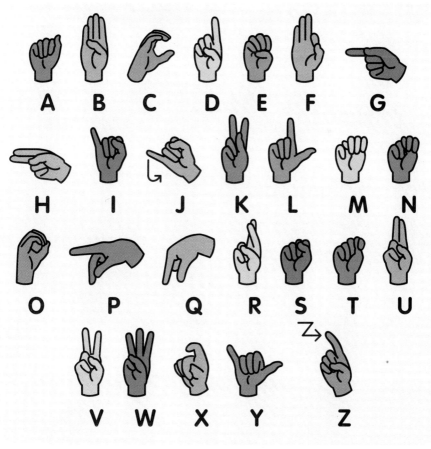

A B C D E F G

H I J K L M N

O P Q R S T U

V W X Y Z

Braille Alphabet and Braille Numbers

a	b	c	d	e	f	g	h	i	j
1	2	3	4	5	6	7	8	9	0

k	l	m	n	o	p	q	r	s	t

u	v	w	x	y	z	Capital Sign	Numeral Sign

Roman Numerals

1	I	6	VI	11	XI
2	II	7	VII	12	XII
3	III	8	VIII	50	L
4	IV	9	IX	100	C
5	V	10	X	1,000	M

Saying Hello and Good-Bye

This table will help you say "hello" and "good-bye" in different languages.

Language	Hello or Good Day	Good-Bye
Chinese (Mandarin dialect)	dzău	dzàijyàn
Farsi (Iran)	salaam سلام	khoda hafez خدا حافظ
French	bonjour	au revoir
German	Guten Tag	Auf Wiedersehen
Hebrew	shalom	shalom
Spanish	hola	adiós
Swahili	neno la kusalimu rafiki au mtani	kwa heri

Animal Facts

Animal	Male	Female	Young	Group
Bear	He-bear	She-bear	Cub	Sleuth
Cat	Tom	Queen	Kitten	Clutter/Clowder
Cattle	Bull	Cow	Calf	Drove/Herd
Chicken	Rooster	Hen	Chick	Brood/Flock
Deer	Buck	Doe	Fawn	Herd
Dog	Dog	Bitch	Pup	Pack/Kennel
Donkey	Jack	Jenny	Foal	Herd/Pace
Duck	Drake	Duck	Duckling	Brace/Herd
Elephant	Bull	Cow	Calf	Herd
Fox	Dog	Vixen	Cub/Kit	Skulk
Goat	Billy	Nanny	Kid	Tribe/Herd
Goose	Gander	Goose	Gosling	Flock/Gaggle
Horse	Stallion	Mare	Filly/Colt	Herd
Lion	Lion	Lioness	Cub	Pride
Monkey	Male	Female	Boy/Girl	Band/Troop
Rabbit	Buck	Doe	Bunny	Nest/Warren
Sheep	Ram	Ewe	Lamb	Flock/Drove
Swine	Boar	Sow	Piglet	Litter/Herd
Whale	Bull	Cow	Calf	Gam/Pod/Herd

Animal Speeds

These speeds are for short distances. For example, a human could not run 28 miles in one hour. However, for a short time, someone could reach that speed.

MILES PER HOUR	1	10	20	30	40	50	60	70	80
Osprey (flies)									80
Cheetah								70	
Quarter Horse						47			
Coyote					43				
Ostrich (runs)					40				
Greyhound					39				
Giraffe				32					
White-tailed Deer				30					
Grizzly Bear				30					
Cat				30					
Human				28					
Elephant			25						
Snake			20						
Giant Tortoise	.17								
Snail	.03								

Measurements

Here are the basic units in the United States system of measurement.

Length (how far)

1 inch (in.) ⸺⸺⸺⸺ ◄········ one inch

1 foot (ft.) = **12 inches**

1 yard (yd.) = **3 feet** = **36 inches**

1 mile (mi.) = **1,760 yards** = **5,280 feet** = **63,360 inches**

Weight (how heavy)

1 ounce (oz.)

1 pound (lb.) = **16 ounces**

1 ton = **2,000 pounds** = **32,000 ounces**

Capacity (how much something can hold)

1 teaspoon (tsp.)

1 tablespoon (tbsp.) = **3 teaspoons**

1 cup (c.) = **16 tablespoons**

1 pint (pt.) = **2 cups**

1 quart (qt.) = **2 pints** = **4 cups**

1 gallon (gal.) = **4 quarts** = **8 pints** = **16 cups**

Metric System

Here are some common metric measures.

Length (how far)

1 millimeter (mm) .   millimeter

10 millimeters

1 centimeter (cm) = **10 millimeters** _____

1 meter (m) = **100 centimeters** = **1,000 millimeters**

1 kilometer (km) = **1,000 meters** =
     100,000 centimeters = **1,000,000 millimeters**

Weight (how heavy)

1 gram (g)

1 kilogram (kg) = **1,000 grams**

Capacity (how much something can hold)

1 milliliter (ml)

1 liter (l) = **1,000 milliliters**

Our Solar System

The nine planets in our solar system orbit around the sun.

Mercury has the shortest year. It is 88 days long.

Venus spins the slowest. It takes 243 days to spin around once.

Earth supports life for plants, animals, and people.

Mars has less gravity than Earth. A 50-pound person would weigh about 19 pounds on Mars.

Jupiter is the largest planet. It is more than 10 times bigger than Earth.

Saturn has seven rings. It also has the most moons—23.

Uranus has the most rings—15.

Neptune is the coldest planet.

Pluto is the smallest planet.

Sun

Mercury   Venus

Earth   Mars

Jupiter

Saturn

Uranus

Neptune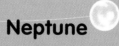

Pluto

All About Maps

Maps help you in many ways. For example, a school map helps you find your way in a new school. A weather map can tell you if you need to wear a coat today.

Around the World

The maps in this chapter help you learn about places in the world and in our country. You will also learn how to read maps, plus much more.

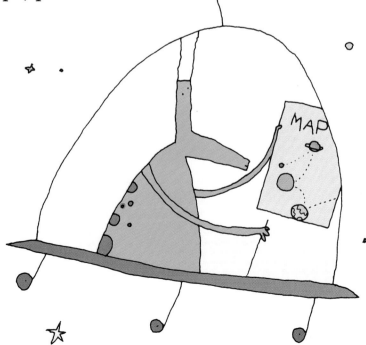

The Compass Rose

Most maps have a **compass rose** to show the four directions: north, south, east, and west. In fact, the compass rose is sometimes called the direction finder.

If a map does not have a compass rose, north is probably at the top of the page, and south is at the bottom. East is to the right of the page, and west is to the left.

Map Key and Symbols

The **key** is a list that explains the symbols used on a map. Symbols are like little signs that tell what is on a map. Here is the key for the map on page 305 in your handbook.

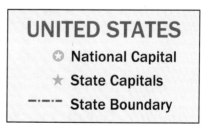

Three **symbols** are listed in this key. There is a symbol for the national capital (☉), for the state capitals (★), and for the state boundaries (----).

The Globe

The best map of the world is a globe. A **globe** shows our earth as it really is: round!

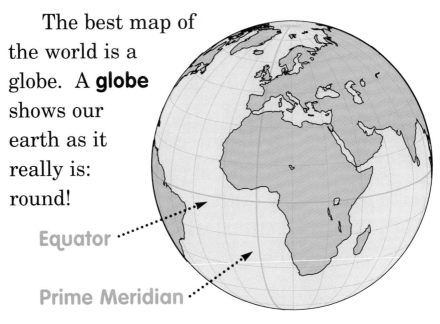

Equator

Prime Meridian

Lines of Latitude and Longitude

Lines of **latitude** go around the globe. The **equator** is the most famous line of latitude. It goes around the middle of the globe.

Lines of **longitude** go up and down, from the North Pole to the South Pole. The **prime meridian** is the most famous line of longitude. It passes through Greenwich, England.

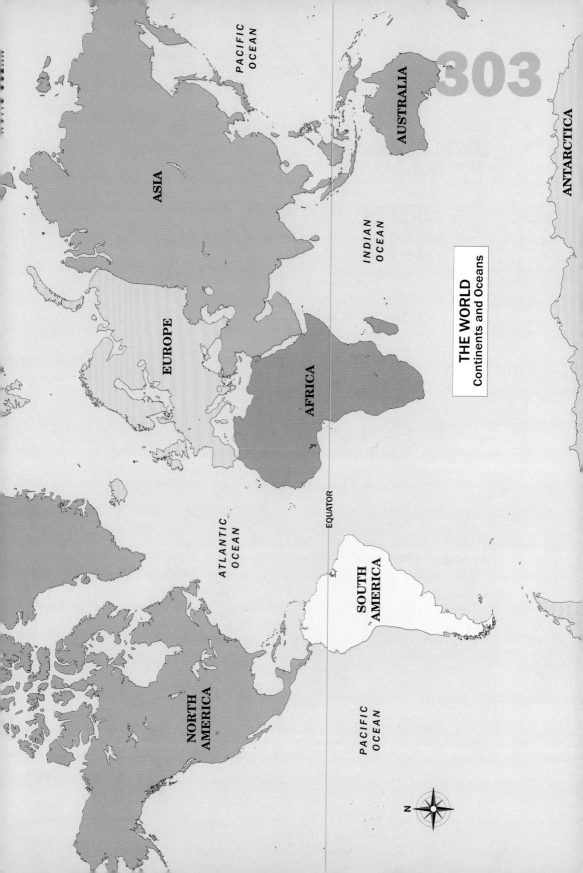

THE WORLD
Continents and Oceans

PACIFIC OCEAN

AUSTRALIA

ASIA

ANTARCTICA

INDIAN OCEAN

EUROPE

AFRICA

ATLANTIC OCEAN

EQUATOR

SOUTH AMERICA

NORTH AMERICA

PACIFIC OCEAN

N

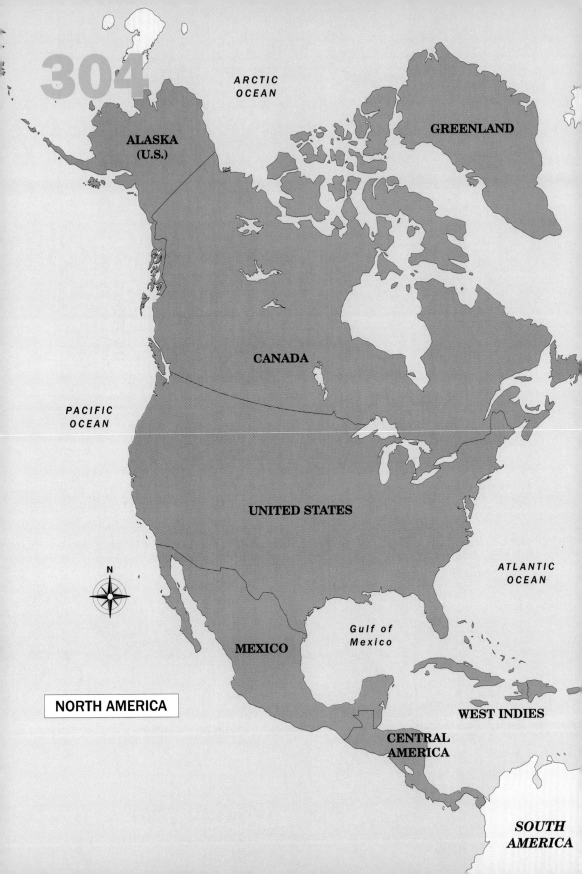

ARCTIC
OCEAN

ALASKA
(U.S.)

GREENLAND

CANADA

PACIFIC
OCEAN

N

UNITED STATES

ATLANTIC
OCEAN

MEXICO

Gulf of
Mexico

NORTH AMERICA

WEST INDIES

CENTRAL
AMERICA

SOUTH
AMERICA

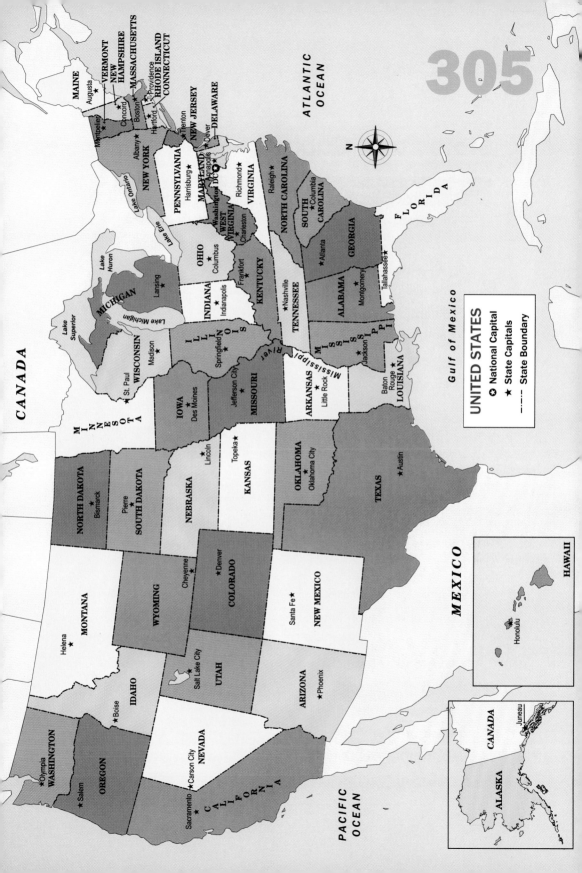

States and Capitals

State	Capital		State	Capital
Alabama	Montgomery		Montana	Helena
Alaska	Juneau		Nebraska	Lincoln
Arizona	Phoenix		Nevada	Carson City
Arkansas	Little Rock		New Hampshire	Concord
California	Sacramento		New Jersey	Trenton
Colorado	Denver		New Mexico	Santa Fe
Connecticut	Hartford		New York	Albany
Delaware	Dover		North Carolina	Raleigh
Florida	Tallahassee		North Dakota	Bismarck
Georgia	Atlanta		Ohio	Columbus
Hawaii	Honolulu		Oklahoma	Oklahoma City
Idaho	Boise		Oregon	Salem
Illinois	Springfield		Pennsylvania	Harrisburg
Indiana	Indianapolis		Rhode Island	Providence
Iowa	Des Moines		South Carolina	Columbia
Kansas	Topeka		South Dakota	Pierre
Kentucky	Frankfort		Tennessee	Nashville
Louisiana	Baton Rouge		Texas	Austin
Maine	Augusta		Utah	Salt Lake City
Maryland	Annapolis		Vermont	Montpelier
Massachusetts	Boston		Virginia	Richmond
Michigan	Lansing		Washington	Olympia
Minnesota	St. Paul		West Virginia	Charleston
Mississippi	Jackson		Wisconsin	Madison
Missouri	Jefferson City		Wyoming	Cheyenne

Facts About the United States

LARGEST STATE
Alaska   586,412 square miles

SMALLEST STATE
Rhode Island   1,214 square miles

LARGEST CITY
New York City   7,322,564 people

LONGEST RIVER
Mississippi River   2,470 miles long

LARGEST LAKE
Lake Superior   31,820 square miles

LARGEST DESERT
Mojave Desert in California
15,000 square miles

HIGHEST POINT
Mt. McKinley in Alaska
20,320 feet above sea level

LOWEST POINT
Death Valley in California
282 feet below sea level

Working with Math

You use math a lot. You add and subtract numbers, you count money, and you tell time. You also measure things, and so on.

From Adding to Telling Time

This chapter will help you become "math smart." The first part shows you how to solve word problems. The second part gives helpful math tables and charts.

Word Problems

Word problems are like little stories. (Some teachers call them story problems.) But they do not have endings. You make the endings by solving the problems!

Example Word Problem

Suzanne has 2 bags of cookies. Each bag has 3 cookies inside. Suzanne's brother gives her another bag with 3 cookies inside. How many cookies does Suzanne have in all?

Fun Learning

Word problems like this one are fun to solve—if you know how to do it! We will show you how on the next two pages.

Solving Word Problems

 1 **Read the problem carefully.**
Look for important words such as "how many" and "in all."

> **How many cookies does Suzanne have in all?**

- If you don't understand part of the problem, ask for help.

 2 Decide what to do.
- Do you have to add or subtract some numbers?
- Or do you have to do two things—maybe add and then subtract?

3 **Do the problem.** Decide how you will solve the problem. You could draw pictures, use counters, or write a math problem.

Counters

● ● ● + ● ● ● + ● ● ● = 9

Math Problem

3 cookies	6 cookies
+ 3 cookies	+ 3 cookies
6 cookies	9 cookies

4 **Check your answer.** Start with your answer and work backward.

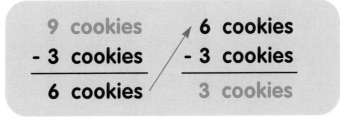

9 cookies	6 cookies
- 3 cookies	- 3 cookies
6 cookies	3 cookies

● Or solve the problem a different way. You should get the same answer.

Math Tables and Charts

Addition Facts

Pick a number at the beginning of a row (4). Pick a number at the top of a column (7). Find your answer where the row and column meet (4) + (7) = (11).

+	1	2	3	4	5	6	7	8	9	10
1	2	3	4	5	6	7	8	9	10	11
2	3	4	5	6	7	8	9	10	11	12
3	4	5	6	7	8	9	10	11	12	13
4	5	6	7	8	9	10	11	12	13	14
5	6	7	8	9	10	11	12	13	14	15
6	7	8	9	10	11	12	13	14	15	16
7	8	9	10	11	12	13	14	15	16	17
8	9	10	11	12	13	14	15	16	17	18
9	10	11	12	13	14	15	16	17	18	19
10	11	12	13	14	15	16	17	18	19	20

Skip Counting

2's	2	4	6	8	10	12	14	16
3's	3	6	9	12	15	18	21	24
4's	4	8	12	16	20	24	28	32
5's	5	10	15	20	25	30	35	40

Place Value Chart

Here are the place values for 3,752:

3	,	7	5	2
thousands	,	hundreds	tens	ones

3 in the thousands' place is **3,000**

7 in the hundreds' place is **700**

5 in the tens' place is **50**

2 in the ones' place is **2**

You read this four-digit number as **three thousand seven hundred fifty-two.**

Fractions

A **fraction** is a part of something. A fraction has a top number and a bottom number, like this example:

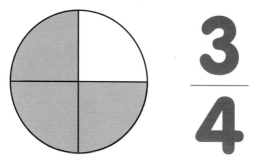

Reading Fractions

The bottom number (4) tells you the circle is divided into four equal parts. The top number (3) tells you that three of the parts are being named. You read 3/4 as **three-fourths**.

More Examples

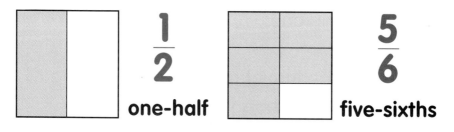

Counting Money

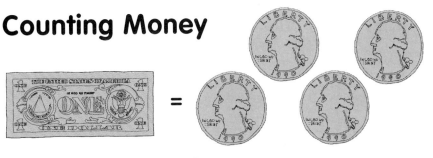

one dollar = four quarters

one quarter = two dimes + one nickel

one dime = two nickels

one nickel = five pennies

How much money?

If you counted all the money shown above, you would have two dollars and eighty cents. You would write $2.80.

Telling Time

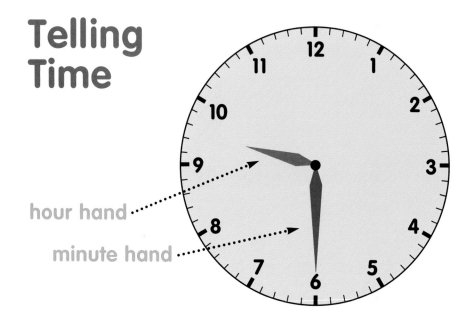

hour hand ....
minute hand ....

one hour = 60 minutes
one-half hour = 30 minutes

2:00

When the minute hand (long hand) is on 12, you write 00 for the minutes.

3:25

When the minute hand is on a number, count by 5's from the top to tell the time. (5, 10, 15, 20, **25**)

3:26

When the minute hand is between numbers, count by 5's from the top. Then add the minute marks past the last number to find the time. (25 + 1 = **26**)

Improving Handwriting

Do you use manuscript or cursive letters? You will find charts for both types of letters in this chapter. The checklist and tips on the last page will help you write neatly.

manuscript

My name is Al.

cursive

My name is Al.

Manuscript Letters

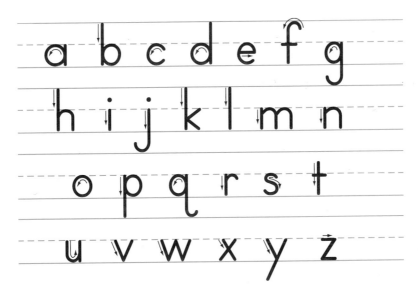

Cursive Letters

Handwriting T|PS

SIT up straight when you write.

HOLD your pencil comfortably, not too tightly.

USE your best handwriting for final copies.

Handwriting Checklist

 Are my letters formed correctly?

 Do all my letters slant the same way?

 Do I have enough space between words?

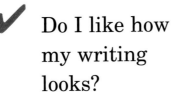 Do I like how my writing looks?

History in the Making

When the Pilgrims arrived in 1620, there were many tribes of people (Native Americans) living in this land that is now the United States. These people had lived here for thousands of years. Each tribe had a way of life related to where it lived.

Native American Regions

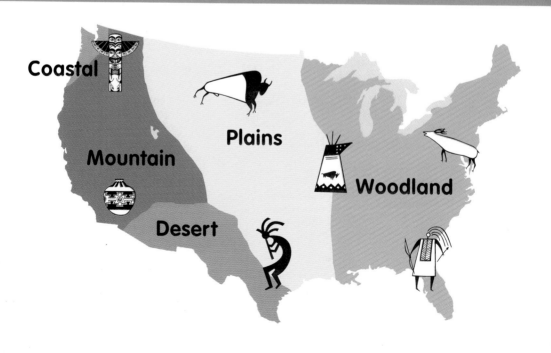

U.S. History

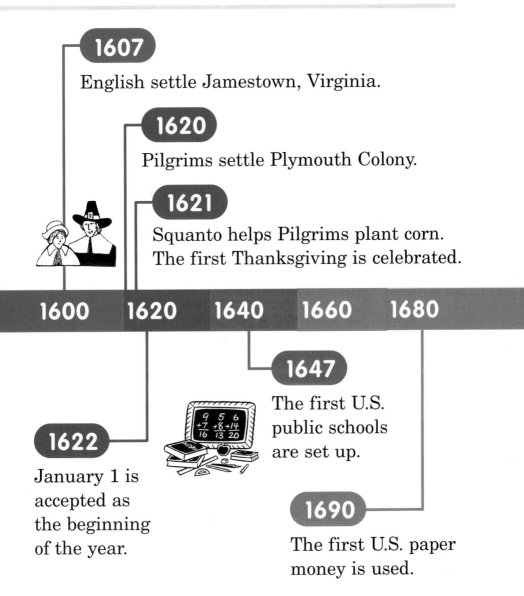

1607
English settle Jamestown, Virginia.

1620
Pilgrims settle Plymouth Colony.

1621
Squanto helps Pilgrims plant corn.
The first Thanksgiving is celebrated.

| 1600 | 1620 | 1640 | 1660 | 1680 |

1647
The first U.S.
public schools
are set up.

1622
January 1 is
accepted as
the beginning
of the year.

1690
The first U.S. paper
money is used.

Discoveries and Daily Life

U.S. History

1733

The thirteen colonies are formed.

1731

Benjamin Franklin begins the first library.

1749

The U.S. population is close to 1,000,000.

| 1700 | 1710 | 1720 | 1730 | 1740 |

1736

The first American cookbook is written.

1704

The first newspaper is written in Boston.

1742

Benjamin Franklin invents the Franklin stove.

Discoveries and Daily Life

1750
Covered wagons begin carrying settlers west.

1789
George Washington is elected first president.

1776
The Declaration of Independence is signed.

1750	1760	1770	1780	1790

1782
The eagle becomes U.S. symbol.

1750
Benjamin Franklin discovers electricity.

1786
The first ice-cream company is founded.

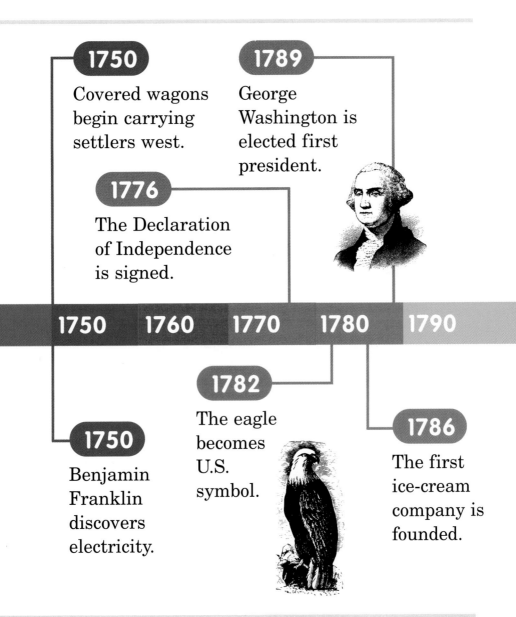

U.S. History

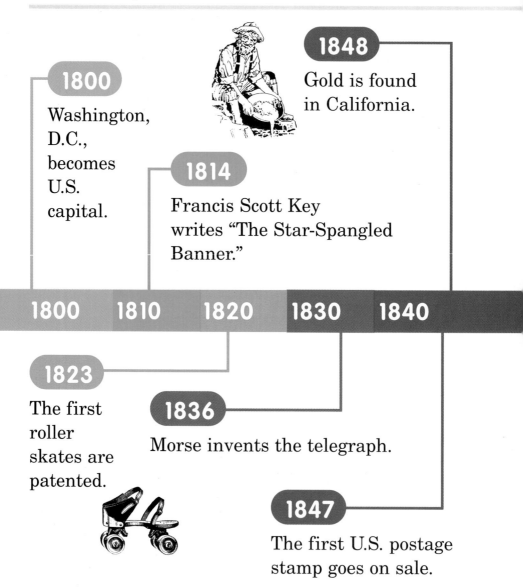

1848
Gold is found in California.

1800
Washington, D.C., becomes U.S. capital.

1814
Francis Scott Key writes "The Star-Spangled Banner."

1800	1810	1820	1830	1840

1823
The first roller skates are patented.

1836
Morse invents the telegraph.

1847
The first U.S. postage stamp goes on sale.

Discoveries and Daily Life

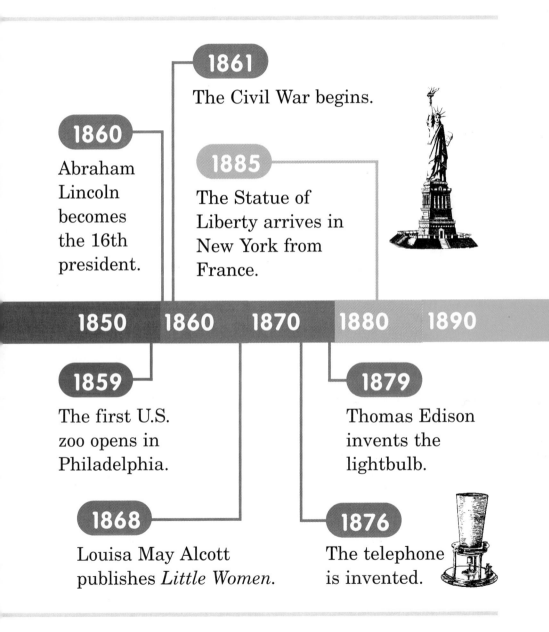

1861
The Civil War begins.

1860
Abraham Lincoln becomes the 16th president.

1885
The Statue of Liberty arrives in New York from France.

1850 1860 1870 1880 1890

1859
The first U.S. zoo opens in Philadelphia.

1868
Louisa May Alcott publishes *Little Women*.

1879
Thomas Edison invents the lightbulb.

1876
The telephone is invented.

U.S. History

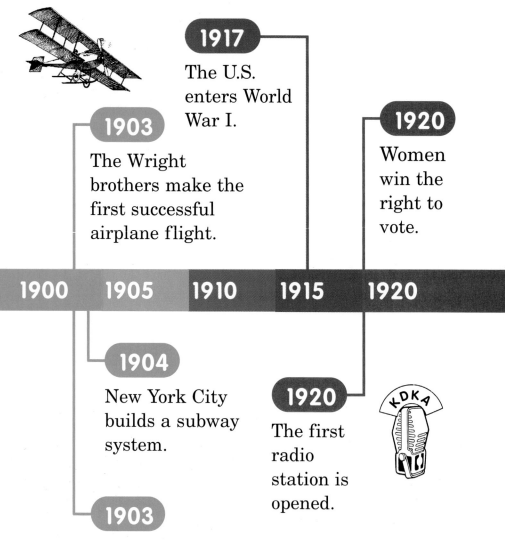

1917
The U.S. enters World War I.

1903
The Wright brothers make the first successful airplane flight.

1920
Women win the right to vote.

1900   1905   1910   1915   1920

1904
New York City builds a subway system.

1920
The first radio station is opened.

1903
The first baseball World Series is played.

Discoveries and Daily Life

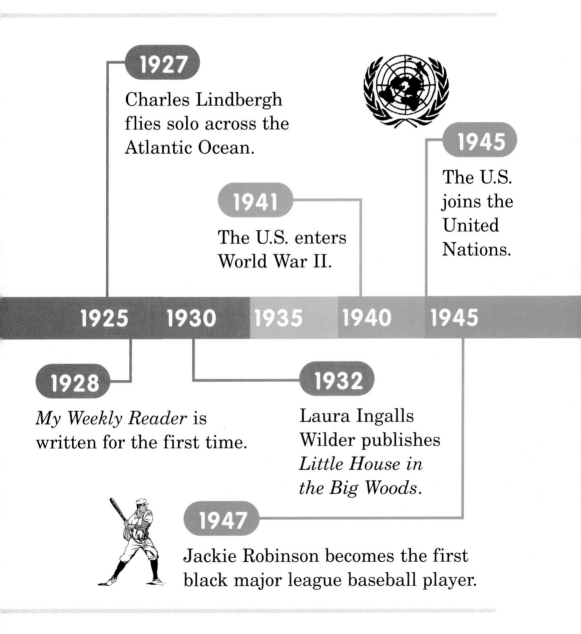

1927

Charles Lindbergh flies solo across the Atlantic Ocean.

1945

The U.S. joins the United Nations.

1941

The U.S. enters World War II.

1925 **1930** **1935** **1940** **1945**

1928

My Weekly Reader is written for the first time.

1932

Laura Ingalls Wilder publishes *Little House in the Big Woods*.

1947

Jackie Robinson becomes the first black major league baseball player.

U.S. History

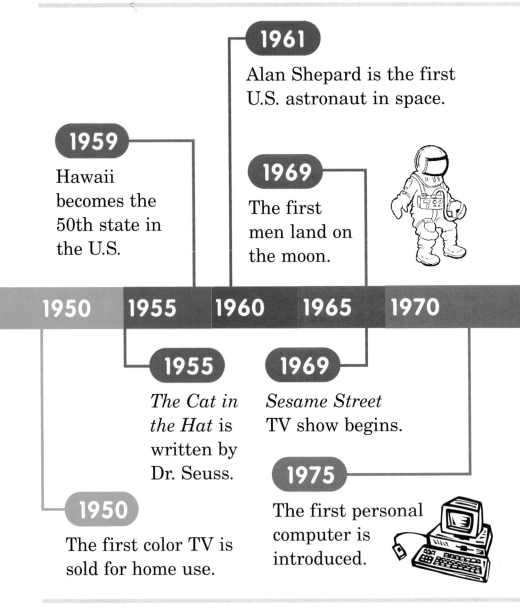

1961
Alan Shepard is the first U.S. astronaut in space.

1959
Hawaii becomes the 50th state in the U.S.

1969
The first men land on the moon.

1950   1955   1960   1965   1970

1955
The Cat in the Hat is written by Dr. Seuss.

1969
Sesame Street TV show begins.

1950
The first color TV is sold for home use.

1975
The first personal computer is introduced.

Discoveries and Daily Life

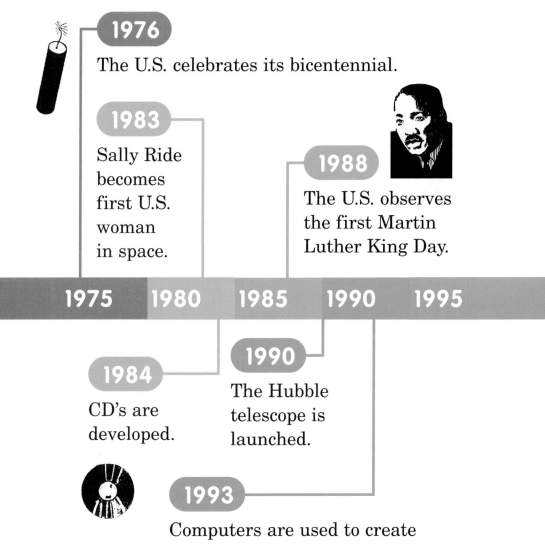

1976

The U.S. celebrates its bicentennial.

1983

Sally Ride becomes first U.S. woman in space.

1988

The U.S. observes the first Martin Luther King Day.

1975 1980 1985 1990 1995

1984

CD's are developed.

1990

The Hubble telescope is launched.

1993

Computers are used to create special effects in *Jurassic Park*.

Index

The **index** helps you find information in your handbook. Let's say you want to learn how to write a poem. You can look in your index under "poetry" for help.

A

B

C

D